Sleepytown Days

Sedgewood® Press
New York

Trice -

Friendship is a chain of gold;
Each link a story to be told.

Tales of rainbows to be seen
Through laughter, tears and unsung dreams.

Yesterday's moments, tomorrows to share --
Link together the friends who care.

This special gift to you we send
The gift of love to you, our friend.

For Sedgewood® Press
Editorial Director: ELIZABETH P. RICE
Associate Editor: LESLIE GILBERT
Production Manager: BILL ROSE

For The Vanessa-Ann Collection

Owners: JO BUEHLER and TERRECE WOODRUFF
Editors: MARGARET MARTI and HEATHER HALES
Art Director: TRICE BOERENS
Needlework Director: NANCY WHITLEY
Finishing Directors: SUSAN WHITELOCK and
    TAMI STEVENS
Layout Director: JULIE TRUMAN
Graphing Director: SUSAN JORGENSEN
Operations Director: KAREN GARDINER
Comptroller: KATIE PEARCE
Customer Relations: PAM RANDALL
Administrative Assistant: BARBARA MILBURN
Photographer: BRENT HERRIDGE

We also wish to acknowledge the contributions of
LORI WARD and SCOTT READ.

Published by SEDGEWOOD® PRESS

Distributed by Macmillan Publishing Company, a division of
Macmillan, Inc.

First Printing 1986
Library of Congress Catalog number: 85-50547
ISBN: 0-02-621560-8
All Rights Reserved.

Printed in the United States of America.

Sleepytown Days

From Sleepytown days

spent in warm summer sun,

To snowflakes falling 'til day is done;

Springtime greetings and autumn gold,

With passing seasons a year unfolds.

The months all bring their own special joy

With lasting treasures for each girl and boy.

Magical friends visit all through the day,

Inside and outside, for hours of play.

Magic is made for starry night dreams

Of gumdrops, rainbows,

and silver moonbeams.

Contents

$\mathcal{A}$ sleepytown sampler

Cover sample: Stitched on Pistachio Hardanger 22 over two threads. Finished design size is 10⅝" x 15¼". Cut fabric 17" x 21". Finished design sizes using other fabrics are — Aida 11: 10⅝" x 15¼"; Aida 14: 8⅜" x 12"; Aida 18: 6½" x 9¼"; Hardanger 22: 5⅜" x 7⅝".

BATES		DMC	(used for cover sample)
			Step One: Cross-stitch (three strands)
1			White
300		745	Yellow · lt. pale
297		743	Yellow · med.
892		225	Shell Pink · vy. lt.
8		761	Salmon · lt.
66		3688	Mauve · med.
42		309	Rose · deep
104		210	Lavender · med.
128		800	Delft · pale
168		597	Turquoise
149		336	Navy Blue
208		563	Jade · lt.
210		562	Jade · med.
942		738	Tan · vy. lt.
379		840	Beige Brown · med.
397		762	Pearl Gray · vy. lt.
			Step Two: Back Stitch (one strand)
297		743	Yellow · med. (bird feet)
42		309	Rose · deep (unicorn reins, blanket fringe, inside apple)
208		563	Jade · lt. (flower stems on left goose and center lamb, apple stems)
210		562	Jade · med. (flower stems on center goose and lower lamb)
379		840	Beige Brown · med. (boy's hair)
149		336	Navy Blue (all else)
			Step Three: French Knots (one strand)
149		336	Navy Blue
379		840	Beige Brown · med.

Opposite page: Childhood and its very best memories are captured forever here by the needle and thread. The blocks of A Sleepytown Sampler create a cheerful collage and represent the months of the year. Think of the endless small and easy projects waiting to be made from these lighthearted motifs.

A sleepytown sampler

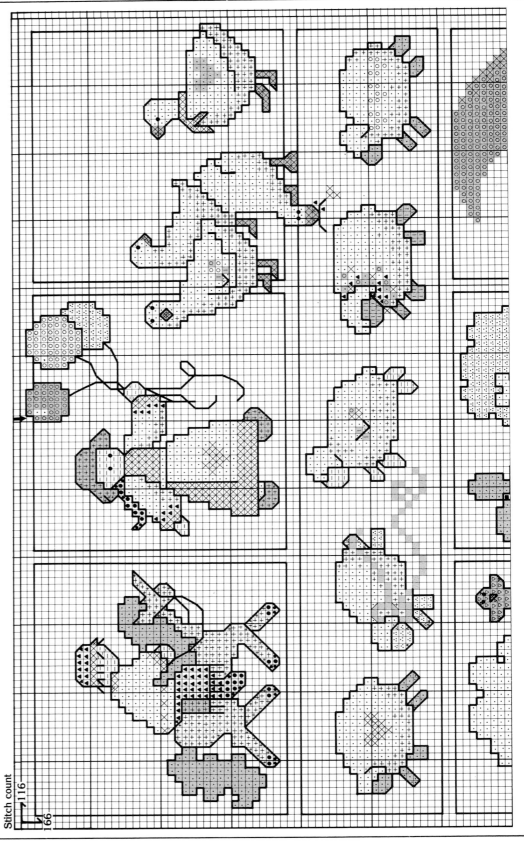

Stitch count
116
166

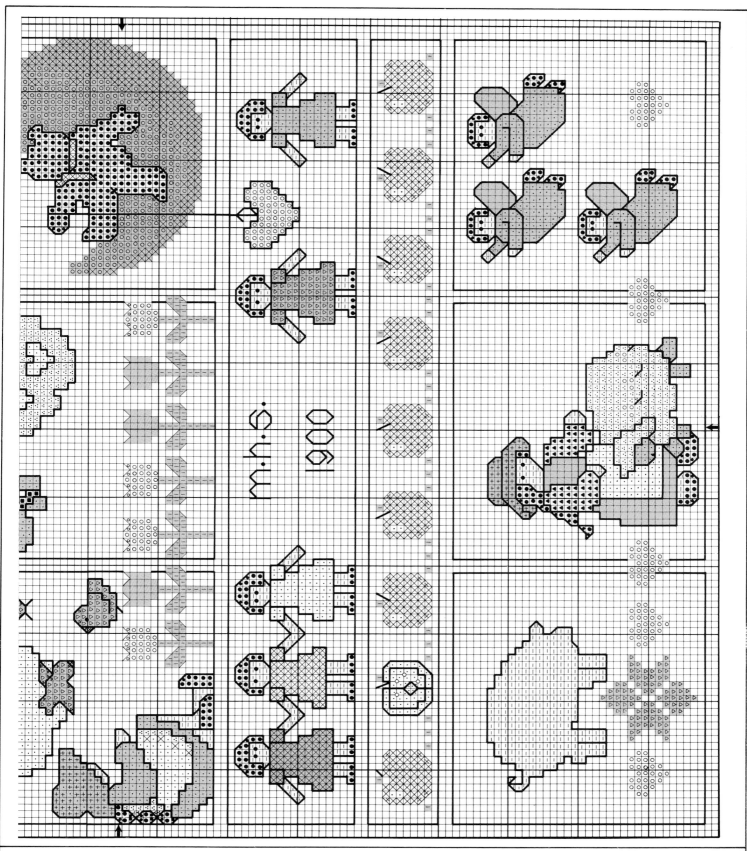

January

January's children are free and rare,
Gentle of nature, handsome and fair.
Unicorns come to offer a ride,
To carry their dreams far and wide.

Graceful and magical, the unicorns in From an Enchanted Forest
are here to make your dreams come true.

Opposite page: Unicorns and more unicorns add their mystical touch to the imaginations of all ages. From an Enchanted Forest is the
cross-stitch work in delicate tones of gray and mauve. The Chintz Unicorns add color and magic to the fantasy. The Little Felt Unicorns,
quickly constructed, enchant playtime hours or charm any Christmas tree.

for Vanessa-Ann
by Tomie dePaola

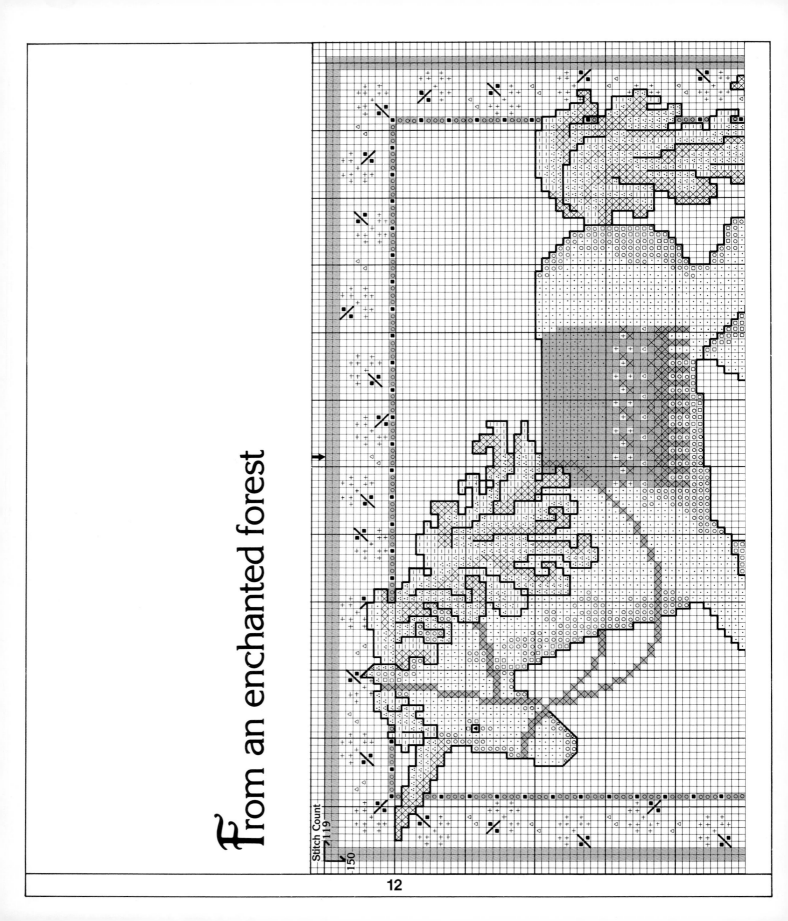

From an enchanted forest

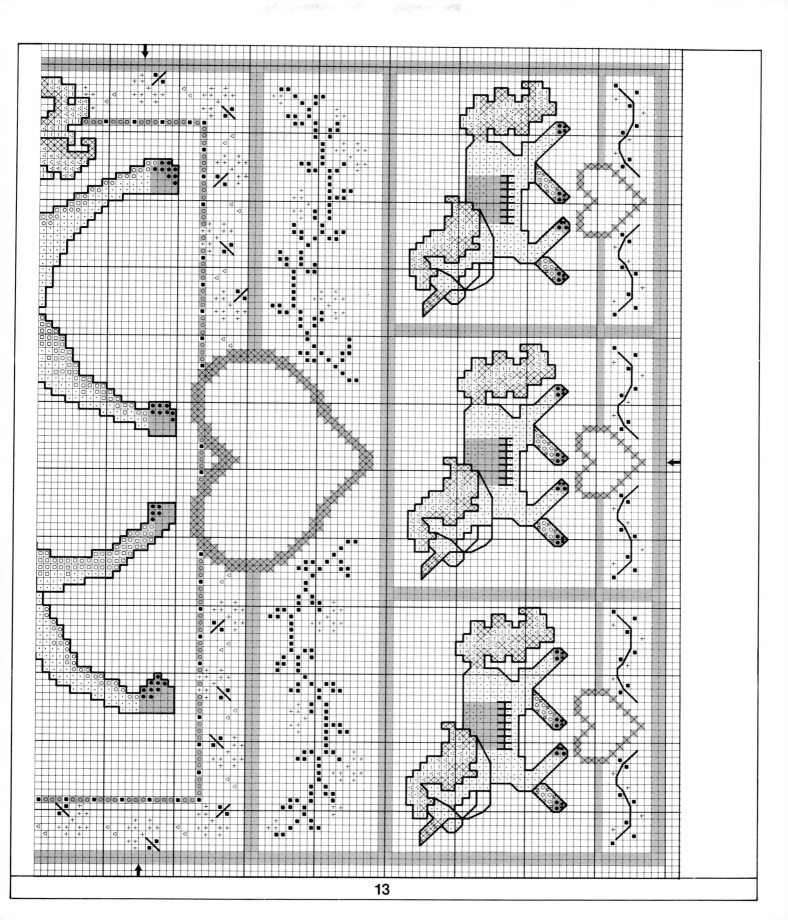

From an enchanted forest

Cover sample: Stitched on White Linen 32 over two threads. Finished design size is 7½" x 9⅜". Cut fabric 14" x 16". Finished design sizes using other fabrics are — Aida 11: 10⅞" x 13⅝"; Aida 14: 8½" x 10¾"; Aida 18: 6⅝" x 8⅜"; Hardanger 22: 5⅜" x 6⅞".

BATES		DMC	(used for cover sample)
			Step One: Cross-stitch (two strands)
366		951	Sportsman Flesh · vy. lt.
968	−	778	Antique Mauve · lt.
893	+	224	Shell Pink · lt.
66	✕	3688	Mauve · med.
869	∴	3042	Antique Violet · lt.
871	✕	3041	Antique Violet · med.
167	○	519	Sky Blue
215	△	368	Pistachio Green · lt.
216	●	367	Pistachio Green · dk.
362		437	Tan · lt.
309	●	435	Brown · vy. lt.
397	·	3072	Beaver Gray · vy. lt.
398	○	453	Shell Gray · lt.
399	▢	452	Shell Gray · med.
905	▲	645	Beaver Gray · vy. dk.
			Step Two: Back Stitch (one strand)
66		3688	Mauve · med. (unicorn's reins, blanket fringe)
216		367	Pistachio Green · dk. (flower stems)
905		645	Beaver Gray · vy. dk. (all else)

Little felt unicorn

Materials needed:
Two 9" x 12" pieces felt; matching thread
1 yd. ⅛" wide satin ribbon; matching thread
Contrasting thread for top stitching on mane and ears
9" x ¼" dowel
Two green star beads (available at craft store)
Stuffing
White glue
Dressmaker's pen
Tracing paper for patterns

A. Prepare fabric:
   1. Make patterns for unicorn head, mane, horn, ear and gusset, transferring all information.
   2. From felt, cut pieces as indicated on patterns.
B. Construct unicorn:
   1. With two mane pieces together, whip stitch scalloped edge. Machine top stitch details shown on pattern. Repeat with both pairs of ear pieces.
   2. With long edges of horn piece together, whip stitch to form cone.
   3. Match one side of gusset to one head piece as indicated on pattern, and whip stitch. Repeat, joining second head piece to second side of gusset.
   4. Insert mane between head pieces. Whip stitch remaining edges, securing mane and leaving bottom edge open.
   5. Stuff top of unicorn head firmly. Insert dowel; stuff around dowel to within 1" of bottom of unicorn.
   6. Tie double thickness of thread securely around neck of unicorn 1" above bottom edge.
   7. Stuff horn. Whip stitch horn and ears to unicorn. Glue star beads for eyes to unicorn.
   8. Cut ribbon into two equal pieces. Tie one around neck of unicorn. With second piece, make halter; see photo and pattern. Tack in place.

FELT
UNICORN

Horn

Cut 1

Ear
Cut 4

FELT UNICORN

Mane

Cut 2

FELT
UNICORN

Gusset

Cut 1

Placement for mane

Placement for gusset

FELT UNICORN

Head

Cut 2

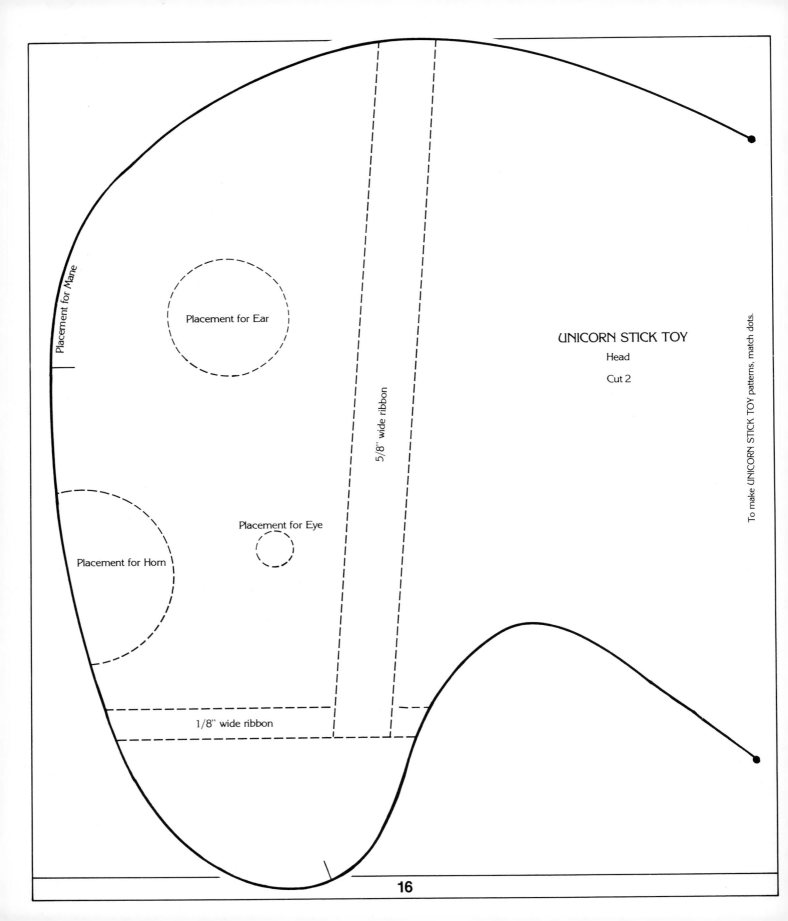

Placement for Mane

Placement for Ear

Placement for Horn

Placement for Eye

5/8" wide ribbon

1/8" wide ribbon

UNICORN STICK TOY

Head

Cut 2

To make UNICORN STICK TOY patterns, match dots.

16

Unicorn stick toy

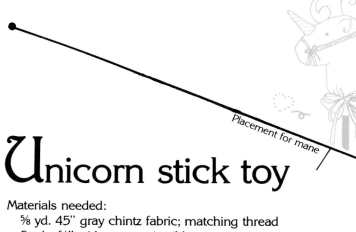

Placement for mane

Materials needed:
⅝ yd. 45" gray chintz fabric; matching thread
5 yds. ⅝" wide gray satin ribbon
5½ yds. ⅛" wide gray satin ribbon
Two ⅜" wide gray buttons for eyes
Charcoal thread
Polyester fleece for mane
Stuffing
One ¾" x 36" wooden dowel
Gray paint
Two ¼" metal eye screws
½ yd. nylon fishing line or kite string
Large-eyed needle
Dressmaker's pen
Tracing paper for patterns

A. Prepare materials:
   1. Make patterns for unicorn head, mane, gusset, horn and ear, transferring all information.
   2. From gray fabric cut head, mane, gusset, horn and ear pieces as indicated.
   3. From fleece, cut one mane.
   4. From ⅝" wide ribbon, cut two 10" lengths. Cut remaining ribbon into three equal lengths.
   5. From ⅛" wide ribbon, cut one 8" piece and two 14" pieces. Cut remaining ribbon into two equal lengths.

   6. Paint dowel gray. Insert two eye screws on opposite sides of dowel 6½" from one end.

B. Construct unicorn:
   1. Mark quilting lines on mane, horn and TWO ear pieces with dressmaker's pen.
   2. Place RIGHT sides of mane pieces together and pin on top of fleece. Stitch around curved outside edge with ¼" seam. Trim fleece close to seam. Clip all seam allowances and trim corners. Turn; baste near seam to secure edge while quilting.
   3. Quilt mane by machine with charcoal thread. Also top stitch ears and horn on pen lines. Set aside.
   4. RIGHT sides of one head piece and gusset together, stitch with ¼" seam on one edge of gusset; back stitch. Repeat with second edge of gusset and second head piece.
   5. Baste each 10" length of ⅝" wide ribbon to RIGHT sides of head as indicated on pattern.
   6. Place mane on RIGHT side of one head piece, raw edges matching; see pattern for placement. Curves of head and mane will be opposite one another. Stitch with ¼" seam, carefully catching all edges and avoiding tucks. RIGHT sides of both head pieces together, stitch around head with ¼" seam, leaving neck open; backstitch. Turn. (Continued)

(Pattern Continued)

UNICORN STICK TOY
(Pattern Continued)

To Make UNICORN STICK TOY patterns, match dots.

7. Make 2" hem around bottom of unicorn neck.

8. RIGHT sides of horn together, match top stitching lines so that when RIGHT side out, they appear to be a spiral. Stitch with ¼" seam, leaving opening as indicated on pattern. Trim point and turn. Turn bottom edge under ¼" and baste. Stuff firmly.

9. RIGHT sides of one ear front (with top stitching lines) and one ear back (without top stitching lines) together, stitch with ¼" seam, leaving opening as indicated on pattern. Trim point and turn. Turn bottom edge under ¼" and stitch with double strand of gathering thread by hand. Stuff firmly. Draw up gathering thread tightly; secure thread. Repeat for second ear.

10. Using double strand of thread, slip stitch horn and ears to unicorn; see pattern for placement. Remove basting thread in horn. Attach buttons for eyes where indicated on pattern.

11. Stuff top half of unicorn head firmly. Insert dowel; eye screws should be near hem line. Continue to stuff firmly, keeping dowel in center of neck, until at hem line.

12. Using large-eyed needle and fishing line or string, stitch gathering thread by hand in ½" stitches around half of neck at hemline then through eye screw. Stitch around second half of neck and through second eye screw. Draw up gathering thread, adjusting stuffing and folds of fabric, until neck of unicorn fits around dowel. Secure line or string.

13. Pin ⅛" wide ribbon around nose with ends under ribbon on one side of head. Tack ends of ⅛" wide ribbon to each other only.

14. Trim ribbon to extend ½" beyond narrow ribbon and fold ends under narrow ribbon. Tack ribbons where they meet on either side of head.

15. Make two bows with 14" lengths of ⅛" wide ribbon. Tack at end of ⅝" wide ribbon; see photo.

16. With three long ⅝" wide ribbons and two long ⅛" wide ribbon, tie bows around neck at gathers. Tack in place.

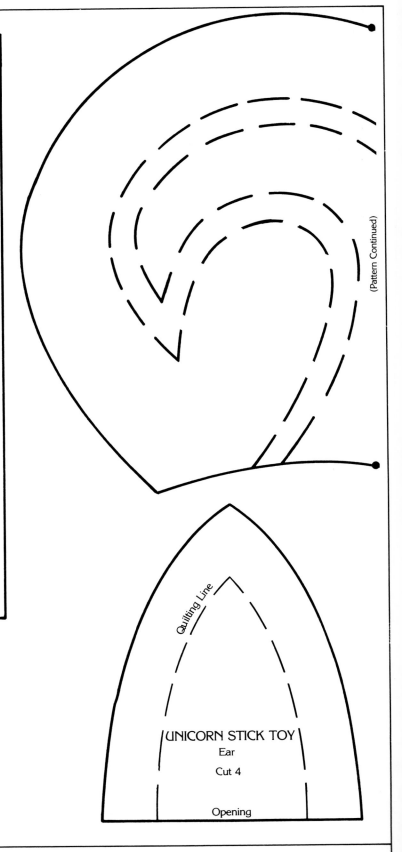

(Pattern Continued)

Quilting Line

UNICORN STICK TOY

Ear

Cut 4

Opening

Unicorn stick toy

(Continued)

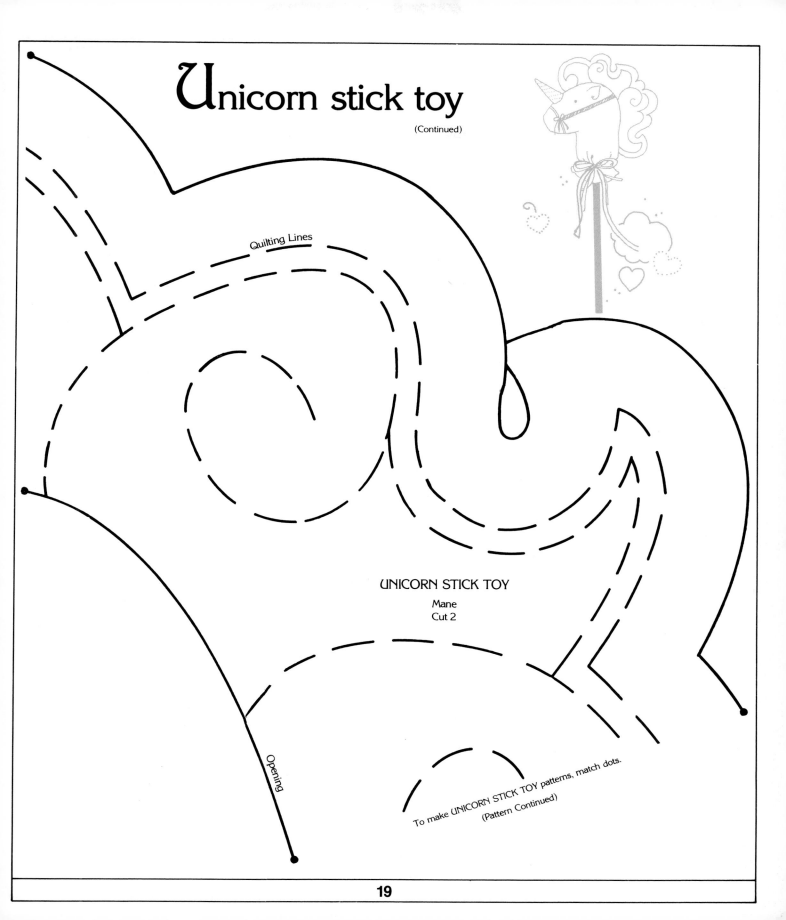

Quilting Lines

UNICORN STICK TOY

Mane
Cut 2

Opening

To make UNICORN STICK TOY patterns, match dots.

(Pattern Continued)

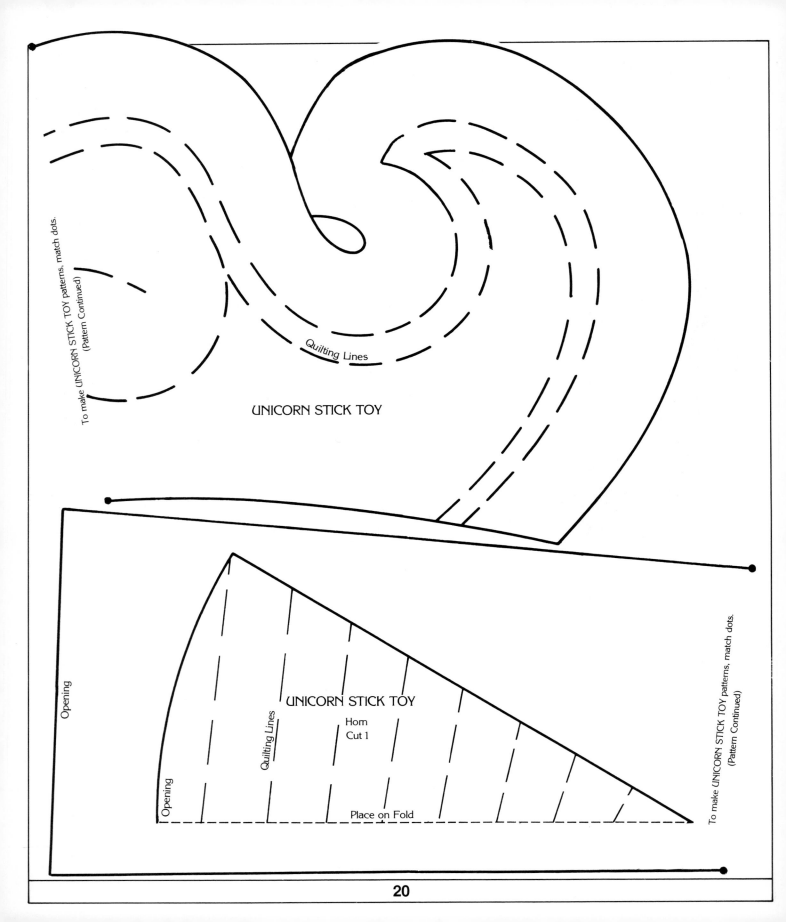

To make UNICORN STICK TOY patterns, match dots. (Pattern Continued)

Quilting Lines

UNICORN STICK TOY

To make UNICORN STICK TOY patterns, match dots. (Pattern Continued)

Opening

Opening

UNICORN STICK TOY

Quilting Lines

Horn
Cut 1

Place on Fold

The Unicorn Stick Toy, ready to act out a plot, waits until the bedtime stories are read.

UNICORN STICK TOY

Gusset

Cut 2

Chintz unicorn

Materials needed:
⅜ yd. 45" white chintz fabric; matching thread
2¾" x 6" piece light blue fabric for saddle; matching thread
1½ yds. ⅛" wide light blue satin ribbon
Polyester fleece
Stuffing
Two blue faceted star beads
Three ½" wide gold metal stars
Pencil or wooden spoon; see Step B7
Dressmaker's pen
Tracing paper for patterns

A. Prepare fabric:
1. Make patterns for unicorn body, gusset, tail, mane, ear and horn, transferring all information.
2. From white fabric, cut body, gusset, ear and horn pieces, as indicated on patterns. Also cut two 6" x 10" pieces to be used for mane and tail.
3. With dressmaker's pen, trace tail and mane patterns completely onto RIGHT side of one 6" x 10" piece.
4. From fleece, cut two 6" x 10" pieces and one 1¾" x 2½" piece for saddle.
B. Construct unicorn:
1. Place two 6" x 10" pieces of fleece between WRONG sides of two 6" x 10" pieces of fabric, baste together. Using blue thread and narrow stitch, machine satin stitch all lines drawn for both pieces; see photo. Trim mane and tail close to outside edge of satin stitching.
2. RIGHT sides of gusset pieces together, stitch upper curved edge with ⅛" seam, twice. Stitch darts in gusset pieces; see pattern.
3. RIGHT sides of one half of gusset and one half of unicorn body together, match legs. Stitch pieces together with ⅛" seam twice. Repeat for second half of gusset and body.

4. Pin mane to RIGHT side of one body piece; see pattern. Curves of head and mane will be opposite one another. Stitch with ⅛" seam, joining mane to one body piece only.
5. RIGHT sides of body pieces together, stitch with ⅛" seam twice, leaving 3" opening in back. Avoid tucks in mane.
6. Place tail between RIGHT sides of body pieces (inside) next to top of gusset; see pattern. Stitch ½" from gusset toward opening with ⅛" seam twice. Turn.
7. Stuff unicorn body firmly. Use small pieces of stuffing and force into legs and head first with eraser end of pencil or handle of wooden spoon. Continue to stuff until very firm. Slip stitch opening closed.
8. RIGHT sides of horn together, stitch with ⅛" seam, leaving bottom open. Turn and stuff firmly. Slip stitch to unicorn head; see pattern.
9. RIGHT sides of two ear pieces together, stitch sides with ⅛" seams, leaving bottom open; turn. Fold ⅛" of raw edges inside and slip stitch opening closed. Pin tuck in ear (see pattern) and slip stitch securely to unicorn head; see pattern. Repeat for second ear.
10. RIGHT sides of blue fabric together, fold to measure 2¾" x 3". Stitch outside edges with ½" seam, leaving 2" opening; clip corners and turn. Insert fleece. Slip stitch opening closed.
11. Cut three 12" pieces of ribbon. Stitch ribbon across saddle, leaving 3" on one edge and 6" on second edge. Tack gold stars to saddle at edge with 3" lengths of ribbon. Place saddle on unicorn. Wrap 6" lengths under unicorn and tie tightly in small bows at gold stars. Trim ends.
12. Glue blue stars for eyes on head; see pattern.
13. Following photo, make reins and bridle with ⅛" wide satin ribbon.

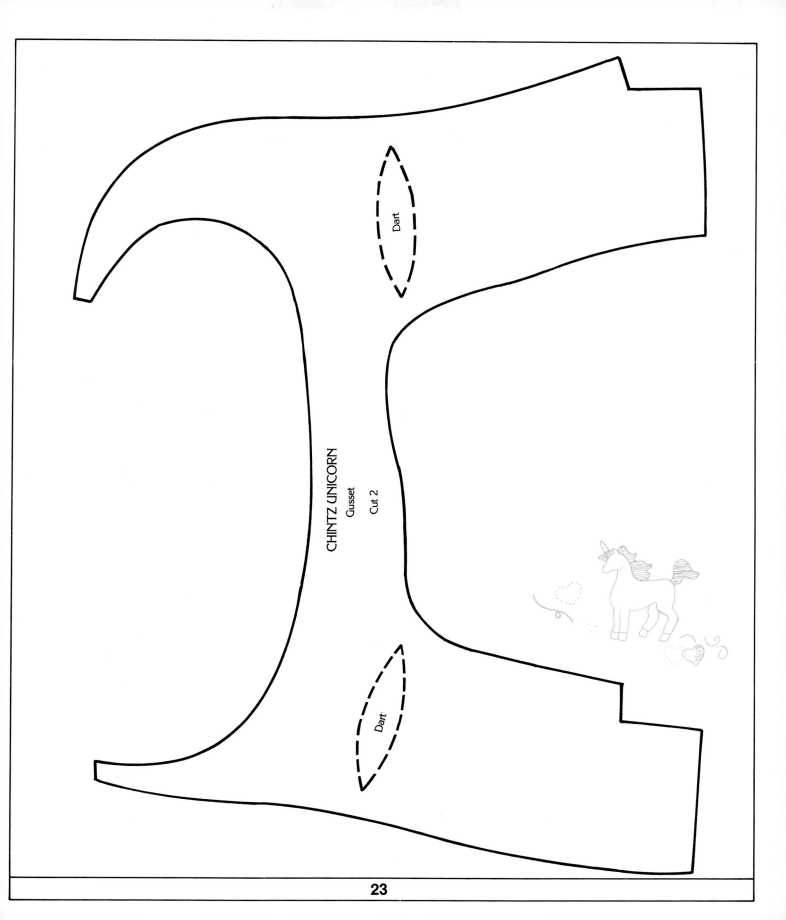

CHINTZ UNICORN

Gusset

Cut 2

Dart

Dart

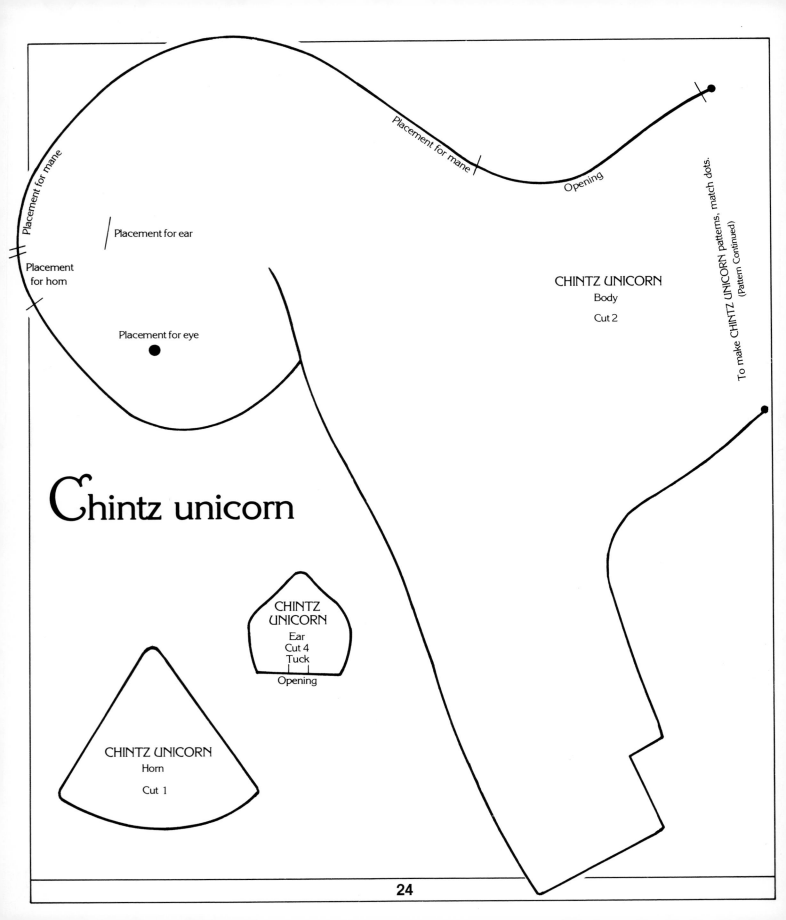

Placement for mane

Placement for mane

Opening

Placement for ear

Placement for horn

Placement for eye

To make CHINTZ UNICORN patterns, match dots.
(Pattern Continued)

CHINTZ UNICORN

Body

Cut 2

Chintz unicorn

CHINTZ
UNICORN

Ear
Cut 4
Tuck

Opening

CHINTZ UNICORN

Horn

Cut 1

Placement
for tail

CHINTZ UNICORN
Tail
Cut 2

CHINTZ
UNICORN

Mane
Cut 2

Gumdrops sweet and hearts growing wild
Are things that make a February child;
Loving friends, days full of fun
And bouncing balloons are for you, little one.

With floppy legs and a ribbon mane, Valentine the Donkey is ready to kick up his heels at the party.

Opposite page: Come to the party! The Dancing Bear Garland, the Wrapped Candies and Valentine the Donkey are ready! The French Friends, dancing their way into one's heart, reflect the gaiety of the occasion. Ready to make party time easier for mother are A Tote for Mother, the Baby Bottle and the Bear Bib. It will be a grand time!

$\mathcal{A}$ tote for mother

All seams are ¼".

Materials needed:
   ½ yd. 45" white fabric; matching thread
   ⅜ yd. 45" pink fabric; matching thread
   ¾ yd. ⅛" wide pink satin ribbon
   Polyester fleece
   Small piece fusing material
   Pink acrylic paint
   Dressmaker's pen
   Tracing paper for pattern
   Stenciling materials; see Stenciling Instructions

A. Prepare fabric:
1. Make fabric heart pattern.
2. Make stencil for stenciled heart; see Stenciling Instructions.
3. From white fabric, cut one 12¼" x 10½" piece for bag back, two 3¾" x 10½" pieces for bag sides, one 3¾" x 12¼" piece for bag bottom and two 3½" x 3½" pieces. Also cut four 1¾" x 22¼" strips for handles. Using dressmaker's pen, mark placement on remaining white fabric for additional 12¼" x 10½" piece and two 3½" x 3½" pieces. Center and trace fabric heart pattern on RIGHT side of 3½" x 3½" pieces.
4. From pink fabric cut two 12¼" x 10½" pieces, two 3¾" x 10½" pieces, and one 3¾" x 12¼" piece for bag lining. Also cut one 12½" x 14¼" piece for pocket section.
5. From fleece, cut two 12¼" x 10½" pieces, two 3¾" x 10½" pieces, one 3¾" x 12¼" piece, one 6¼" x 14¼" piece and two 1¾" x 22¼" strips.
6. From fusing material, cut two 3½" x 3½" pieces.
7. Using pink paint, stencil hearts in center of heart patterns on white fabric. Also stencil hearts in center of heart patterns on white fabric. Also stencil hearts on white fabric with 12¼" x 10½" markings; see Diagram 1 for placement. Set aside.

Diagram 1

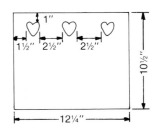

B. Construct bag:
1. Layer one 1¾" x 22¼" fleece strip, then two 1¾" x 22¼" white strips, RIGHT sides together. Stitch long edges; turn. Topstitch ¼" from each edge. Repeat with remaining 1¾" x 22¼" fleece strips and white strips.
2. WRONG sides together, fold pink fabric for pocket section in half to measure 6¼" x 14¼". Place 6¼" x 14¼" fleece piece between pink fabric; pin. Using pink thread, topstitch ¼" from fold. Using dressmaker's pen, mark stitching line 6¼" from and parallel to left edge of pocket section. Mark second stitching line 4" from the first line.
3. Cut one 12¼" x 10½" white piece with stenciling for bag front. Baste corresponding fleece piece to WRONG side of bag front. Fold "pleats" in first pocket of pocket section as shown in Diagram 2; press. Place on RIGHT side of lower edge of bag front, matching raw edges; baste. Using pink thread, stitch on stitching lines for pockets through all layers and topstitch on white fabric around stenciled hearts.

Diagram 2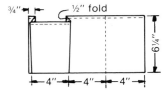

4. Baste corresponding fleece pieces to WRONG sides of remaining white pieces. RIGHT sides together, stitch bag front to 10½" edge of side piece. Repeat with second side piece and opposite edge of bag front. Stitch bag back to remaining raw edges of side pieces. RIGHT sides together and matching corners, stitch bottom piece to bag.
5. Repeat Step B4 using pink pieces and omitting fleece pieces to make lining.
6. RIGHT sides together, place end of one handle ¾" from upper right corner of bag front, matching raw edges; baste. Place second end of handle ¾" from opposite corner of bag front, matching raw edges; baste. Repeat with second handle and bag back.

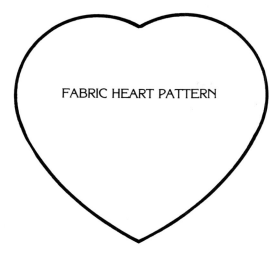

FABRIC HEART PATTERN

7. RIGHT sides of bag and lining together, stitch top of bag, leaving 4" opening. Turn and tuck lining inside. Slip stitch opening closed. Using white thread, top-stitch ¼" from top of bag. Remove basting.

8. Cut 3½" x 3½" white piece with stenciling on pen lines. Pin fusing material to WRONG sides of corresponding stenciled white pieces. Place on WRONG sides of remaining 3½" x 3½" white pieces. Remove pins and fuse according to manufacturer's instructions. Using white thread, machine satin stitch on heart outline. Cut excess fabric close to satin stitching. Knot ribbon 1" from each end. Tack one knot to back of each heart piece. Tie in a bow around bag handle.

Baby bottle

Materials needed:
    7½" x 8½" piece white fabric; matching thread
    Small piece pink fabric; matching thread
    ¾ yd. ⅛" wide pink satin ribbon
    Stuffing
    Fine tip blue marker
    Dressmaker's pen
    Tracing paper for pattern

A. Prepare fabric:
  1. Make circle pattern.
  2. From pink fabric, cut one 2½" x 8½" strip and one 2½" x 1½" piece. Also cut one circle.

B. Construct bottle:
  1. To make nipple, fold 2½" x 1½" pink piece, RIGHT sides together, to measure 1¼" x 1½". Stitch 1½" edge with ¼" seam; turn.
  2. Fold edges of one end of nipple piece ¼" to WRONG side. Stuff firmly from raw edges to fold. Using dress-maker's pen, mark second circle on WRONG side of pink circle ¼" from edge. Clip fabric to pen line at ¼" intervals. Fold clipped edges to WRONG side. Place on folded end of nipple piece; slip stitch. Set aside.
  3. RIGHT sides together, stitch 8½" edges of white and pink pieces with ½" seam. Press seam toward pink fabric.
  4. Fold white with pink piece, RIGHT sides together, to measure 4¼" x 9". Stitch long edge with ½" seam; turn.
  5. Fold edge of white fabric ½" to WRONG side. Sew running stitch ¼" from edge. Pull tightly, secure. Stuff firmly to within 1" of top edge of pink fabric.
  6. Fold edges of pink fabric ½" to WRONG side. Sew running stitch ¼" from edge; do not cut thread. Place nipple in center of bottle top. Pull thread to gather fabric around nipple ½" from raw edges; secure. Tack bottle top to nipple.
  7. Using fine tip marker, trace ounces on bottle; see photo and pattern.
  8. Tie ribbon around bottle in 4" wide bow.

BABY BOTTLE
Circle

BABY BOTTLE
Lettering

···· 3 oz.

···· 2 oz.

···· 1 oz.

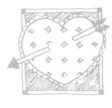

Basket pin cushion

Note: Measurements and amount of fabric used will need to be adjusted according to individual baskets.

Materials needed:
   Wicker basket with handle (5" diameter, 3" high)
   ¾ yd. 45" pink fabric; matching thread
   1¼ yds. 45" white with pink window pane fabric
   10" x 10" piece white fabric; matching thread
   1½ yds. ½" wide pink twill tape
   ⅝ yd. small cording
   Stuffing
   Polyester fleece
   Pink acrylic paint
   Fabric glue
   Dressmaker's pen
   Tracing paper for patterns
   Stenciling materials; see Stenciling Instructions

A. Prepare fabric:
   1. Make 8" and 24" circle patterns; see General Instructions.
   2. Make stencil for heart; see Stenciling Instructions.
   3. From pink fabric, cut one 24" circle for basket cover.
   4. From window pane fabric, cut 4" wide bias strips, piecing as needed, to equal 1 yd.
   5. Using dressmaker's pen, transfer outline of 8" circle on RIGHT side of white fabric. Using pink paint, stencil heart in center of RIGHT side of white fabric with circle. Set aside.
   6. From fleece, cut one 3" x 1¼ yd. strip.
B. Construct pin cushion:
   1. Wrap fleece around outside of basket three times. Tack end to secure.
   2. Stitch one row of gathering thread around pink circle. Center basket on WRONG side of circle. Bring circle up around basket and fleece and tie cording around top of basket to secure fabric; see Diagram 1.

Diagram 1

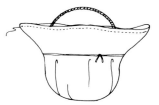

3. Pull gathering thread to fit edge of circle around top of basket, folding WRONG sides together; secure. Tack folds to side of basket to form scallops; see photo.
4. Cut out circle with stenciling. Stitch one row of gathering thread around edge of circle. Place stuffing in center of WRONG side of circle. Pull up gathering thread to form piece for center of basket; secure. Stuff basket. Insert stenciled piece for center; see photo.
5. RIGHT sides together, stitch long sides of bias strip with ¼" seam; turn. Press with seam in center back of strip. Stitch one row of gathering thread ½" from one fold of strip and a second row 1" from opposite fold. Pull up gathering threads to fit strip around basket top, distributing fullness evenly. With edge of smaller gathers up, glue seam side of strip around basket top, folding ends under and tacking strip around bases of handle; see photo.
6. Cut one 40" length of twill tape. Fold into three 5" loops. Using remaining tape, tie loops to basket handle; see photo.

STENCILED
HEART PATTERN

Placement for ribbon ties

Placement for ribbon ties

BEAR BIB PATTERN

Bear bib

Materials needed:
¼ yd. 45" white fabric; matching thread
Small piece pink fabric; matching thread
Small piece brown fabric; matching thread
9" x 9" piece polyester fleece
Small pieces fusing material
2 yds. ⅛" wide white satin ribbon
2 small black bead buttons; matching thread
Pink embroidery floss
Dressmaker's pen
Tracing paper for patterns

A. Prepare fabric:
1. Make pattern for bib; transferring all information. Make patterns for cheeks and nose.
2. From white fabric, cut two 9" x 9" pieces. Using dressmaker's pen, center and transfer outline of bib and all information to RIGHT side of one white piece.
3. From pink fabric, cut two cheek pieces.
4. From brown fabric, cut one nose piece.
5. From fusing material, cut two cheek pieces and one nose piece.
B. Construct bib:
1. Match fusing material to WRONG sides of corresponding cheek and nose pieces, fuse to bib according to manufacturer's instructions. Using matching thread, machine satin stitch around each piece.
2. Layer fleece between WRONG sides of white pieces, placing piece with pattern on top; baste. Using matching white thread, machine satin stitch outline of bib. Trim excess fabric and fleece close to satin stitching. Remove basting. Satin stitch edge again.
3. Using two strands embroidery floss, back stitch mouth; see pattern.
4. Sew on buttons for eyes; see pattern for placement.
5. Cut ribbon into two equal lengths. Tie knot in center of one length. Tack knot to WRONG side of bib; see pattern for placement. Handling both ribbon ends as one, tie second knot 7" from bib. Repeat with remaining length of ribbon.

Dancing bear garland

Materials needed for one bear:
¼ yd. 45" fabric for body; matching thread
Small piece fabric for tie; matching thread
⅜ yd. ⅛" wide pink satin ribbon
Pink embroidery floss
Brown or pink acrylic paint
Small paint brush
Stuffing
Dressmaker's pen
Tracing paper for patterns

Materials needed for garland:
Five completed Dancing Bears
Four completed Wrapped Candies
3½ yds. ⅜" wide pink grosgrain ribbon; matching thread
Thread to match bears

A. Prepare fabric for bear:
1. Make patterns for bear body and tie, transferring all information.
2. From fabric for body, cut one body piece. Using dressmaker's pen, transfer body pattern to RIGHT side of remaining fabric. Using pink or brown paint, paint nose and inside of ears on piece with pattern for bear front.
3. From fabric for tie, cut two tie pieces.
B. Construct bear:
1. RIGHT sides together, stitch tie pieces with ¼" seam, leaving 1" opening. Clip corners; turn. Slip stitch opening closed. Press. Set aside.
2. Using two strands embroidery floss, stitch two French knots for eyes on bear front; cut bear front on outline.
3. RIGHT sides of bear pieces together, stitch with ¼" seam, leaving opening. Clip curves; turn. Stuff firmly. Slip stitch opening closed.
4. Tack tie in place on bear front.
5. Tie ribbon in 2" wide bow around neck.
C. Construct garland:
1. Beginning and ending with a bear, alternate bears and candies on flat surface.
2. With end of candy wrapper around paw, tack candy wrapper to back of paw only. Repeat for remaining bears and candies.
3. Cut ribbon into two equal lengths. Tie each length into 2½" wide bow. Tack one bow to bear paw on each end of garland.

Opening

Tie
Cut 2

DANCING BEAR GARLAND

Body

Cut 2

Valentine the donkey

All seams are ¼".

Materials needed:
    ⅜ yd. 45" fabric; matching thread
    ⅛ yd. 45" pink print fabric; matching thread
    Two ⅛" wide black buttons with shanks; matching thread
    10 yds ⅛" wide pink satin ribbon; matching thread
    ½ yd. ½" wide pink twill tape
    Fusible interfacing
    Stuffing
    Tracing paper for patterns

Prepare fabric:
1. Make patterns for donkey body, leg, ear, foot pad, hoof and two gusset pieces.
2. From brown fabric, cut ear, body, gusset and leg pieces.
3. From pink print fabric, cut ear, hoof and foot pad pieces.
4. From interfacing, cut four hoof pieces. Match to pink hoof pieces and fuse according to manufacturer's instructions. Cut fringe on hooves as indicated on pattern.

B. Construct donkey:
1. Match RIGHT sides of two leg pieces. Stitch pieces together entire length of side.
2. RIGHT sides of one foot pad piece to bottom edge of leg pieces, stitch; see Diagram 1.

Diagram 1

3. Stitch second side of leg pieces, leaving opening as indicated on pattern. Complete pad seam.
4. Repeat Steps B1 through B3 for remaining legs.
5. Match A to A on gusset pieces; stitch. Pin RIGHT side of gusset to one body piece, beginning at B on both pieces. Insert two legs; see pattern for placement. Stitch one side of gusset to body. Repeat for second side of body, leaving opening in rear. Turn; stuff body firmly. Slip stitch opening closed.
6. Stuff legs firmly; slip stitch openings closed.

7. RIGHT sides of one brown and one pink ear piece together, stitch, leaving bottom edge open. Turn. Repeat.
8. Fold raw edges of ears inside; slip stitch. Fold ear in half. Tack ears to head; see pattern for placement.
9. Wrap hooves around feet. Slip stitch edges together. Tack slip stitched edge to back seam of leg.
10. From ribbon, cut one 12" length and five 18" lengths; set aside. To make mane, fold remaining ribbon into two or three 3" wide loops. Tack ribbon to center of gusset at back of neck. Continue to fold and tack ribbon loops to gusset ½" in front of ears.
11. Tie 12" length of ribbon into 4" wide bow. Tack to front of mane.
12. Tie four 18" lengths of ribbon in bows above hooves. Tack bows on front legs seams.
13. To make tail, fold remaining piece of ribbon in half. Tack fold to gusset; see pattern for placement. Twist ribbon ends together and knot. Trim ends.
14. For reins, fold under each end of twill tape. Slip stitch ends to nose with fold in twill tape on seams; see Diagram 2.
15. Sew buttons for eyes to body.

Diagram 2

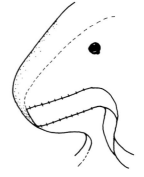

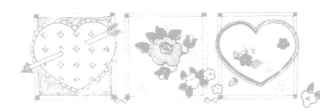

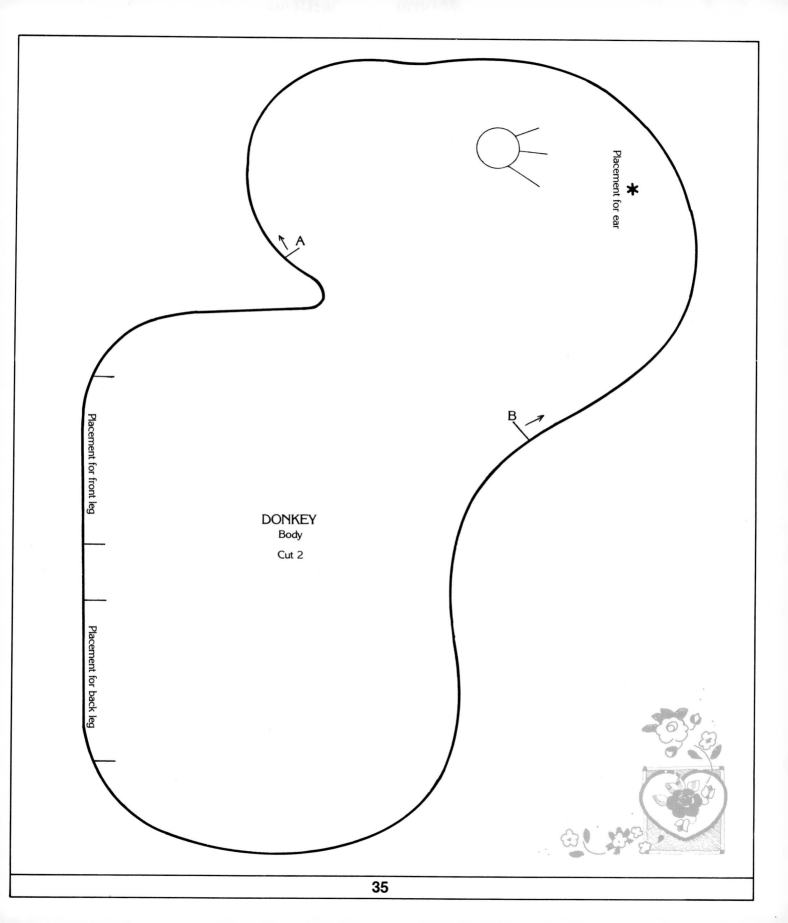

Placement for ear

＊

A

B

Placement for front leg

Placement for back leg

DONKEY
Body

Cut 2

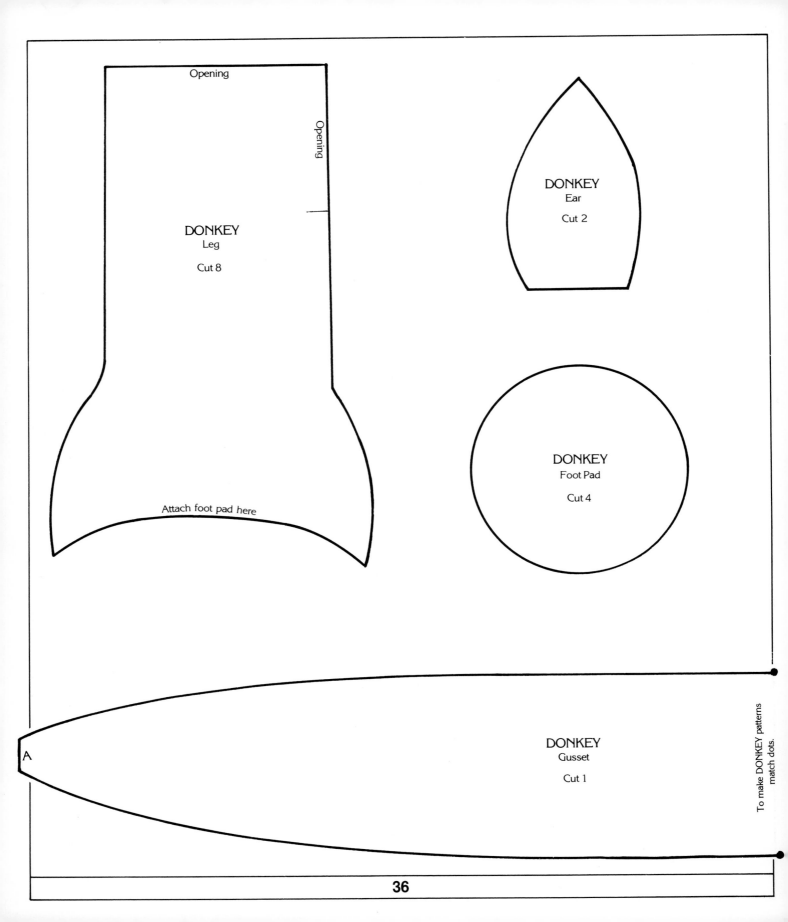

Opening

Opening

DONKEY
Leg

Cut 8

Attach foot pad here

DONKEY
Ear

Cut 2

DONKEY
Foot Pad

Cut 4

A

DONKEY
Gusset

Cut 1

To make DONKEY patterns match dots.

36

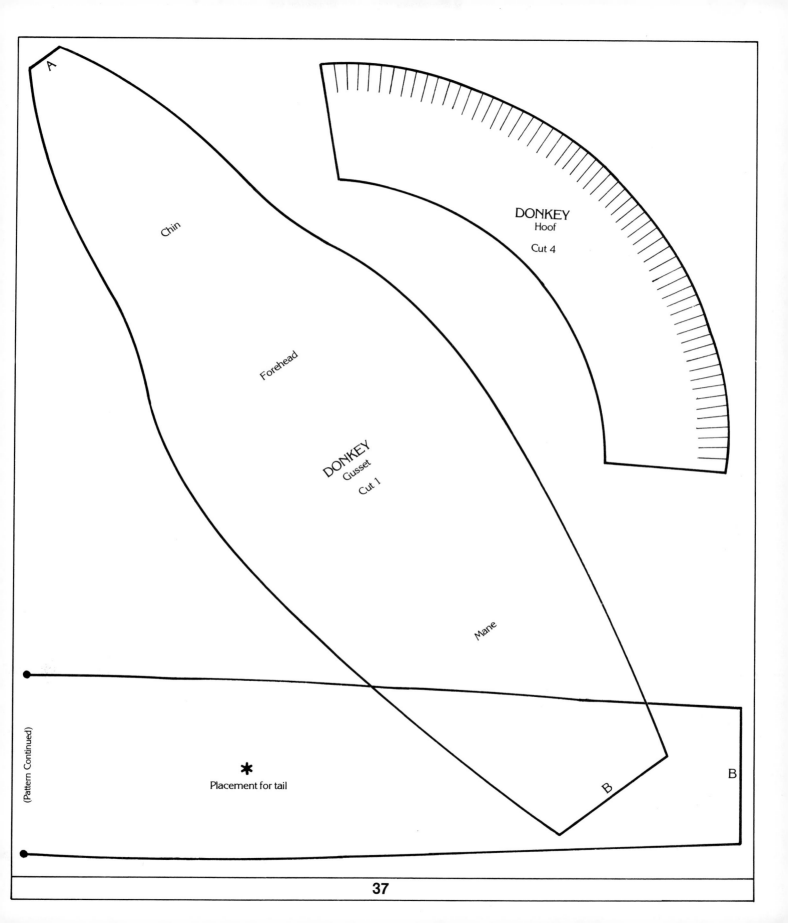

A

Chin

Forehead

DONKEY
Hoof

Cut 4

DONKEY
Gusset

Cut 1

Mane

(Pattern Continued)

✳
Placement for tail

B

B

Wrapped candies

Materials needed for one candy:
- ¼ yd. 45" fabric; matching thread
- ¾ yd. ⅛" wide satin ribbon
- Stuffing
- Finishing option for label: small piece muslin, embroidery floss, dressmaker's pen

1. From fabric, cut two 6½" x 5½" pieces. For shorter, rounder candies, cut two 5½" x 6" pieces.
2. RIGHT sides together, stitch fabric pieces with ¼" seam, leaving 1½" opening in one 6½" end. Clip corners. Turn; slip stitch opening closed.
3. Finishing option for label: Using dressmaker's pen, transfer embroidery patterns for lettering to muslin. Using two strands embroidery floss, backstitch letters. Cut muslin 1½" wide with lettering centered vertically and ½" beyond lettering on each end. Fold all edges ¼" to WRONG side; press. Center on fabric candy wrapper; slip stitch. Using two strands embroidery floss, sew blanket stitch around label.
4. Using matching thread, slip stitch 6" edges of fabric candy wrapper together to form tube.
5. Using double strand of thread, sew running stitch 1" from one end of fabric candy wrapper. Pull thread tightly to gather; secure. Note: To use "butter rum" label, sew running stitch ¾" from end.
6. Stuff firmly to within 1" of second end. Repeat Step 5 on remaining end.
7. Cut ribbon into two equal lengths. Tie each length into 2" wide bow around gathers on each end of candy wrapper.

WRAPPED CANDIES LETTERING PATTERNS

vanilla
butter rum
chocolate
caramel

Opposite page: Nothing feels more like a party than the mystery of unopened gifts. Here the French Friends and the Wrapped Candies await the party's surprises.

the little french folk

French friends

Cover Sample: Stitched on White Linen 32 over two threads. Finished design size is 7½" x 5½". Cut fabric 14" x 12". Finished design sizes using other fabrics are — Aida 11: 10⅞ x 8⅛"; Aida 14: 8½" x 6⅜"; Aida 18: 6⅝" x 5"; Hardanger 22: 5⅜" x 4".

BATES		DMC	(used for cover sample)
			Step One: Cross-stitch (two strands)
1			White
300		745	Yellow · lt. pale
297		743	Yellow · med.
778		948	Peach Flesh · vy. lt.
778		754	Peach Flesh · lt.
8		761	Salmon · lt.
25		3326	Rose · lt.
42		335	Rose
108		211	Lavender · lt.
105		209	Lavender · dk.
128		800	Delft · pale
130		809	Delft
265		3348	Yellow Green · lt.
208		563	Jade · lt.
210		562	Jade · med.
882		407	Sportsman Flesh · dk.
360		898	Coffee Brown · vy. dk.
			Step Two: Back Stitch (one strand)
266		3347	Yellow Green · med. (background flower stems)
210		562	Jade · med. (flower stems on clothing)
882		407	Sportsman Flesh · dk. (boy's hair)
382		3371	Black Brown (all else)
			Step Three: French Knots (one strand)
382		3371	Black Brown

French friends

the little french folk

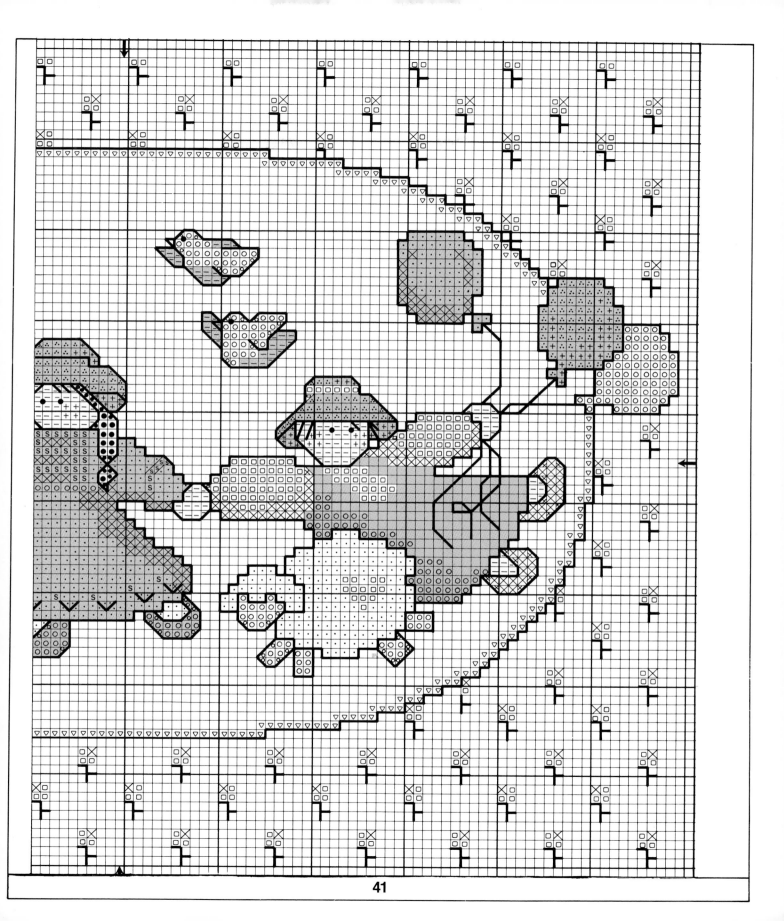

March

Little March children, who so love spring
With feathered friends and wonderful things.
Gather geese as they parade along
And dance to the music of an old goose song.

Rainy spring days are best when spent with My Fine, Feathered Friend.

Opposite page: Inside, where it is dry, awaits A Stenciled Notebook to be filled with photos or momentos. Hanging on the wall, ready to brighten any room, is Gathering The Geese. A Quilted Vest and The Goslings' Bunting, in their bright and cheerful way, warm a March afternoon as My Fine, Feathered Friend looks on.

My fine, feathered friend

Materials needed:
  ½ yd. 45" white with blue dot fabric; matching thread
  ⅛ yd. 45" yellow pin dot fabric for beak and feet; matching thread
  1 yd. ¼" wide yellow satin ribbon
  Small piece blue pin dot fabric for heart
  ¾ yd. small cording
  Stuffing
  Tracing paper for patterns

A. Prepare fabric:
  1. Make patterns for goose body, tail, foot, leg, beak and heart, transferring all information. Note that pattern for goose body is continued onto three pages.
  2. From white/blue fabric, cut body and tail pieces according to patterns.
  3. From yellow pin dot fabric, cut beak, leg and foot pieces according to patterns.
  4. From blue pin dot, cut heart pieces.

B. Construct goose:
  1. WRONG sides of one beak piece together, fold on dotted line. Stitch close to fold making narrow tuck. Repeat with second beak piece.
  2. RIGHT sides of one beak piece and one body piece together, stitch with ¼" seam. Clip curved seam allowance. Repeat.
  3. RIGHT sides of body pieces together, stitch with ¼" seam from neck, around beak and down back through tail.
  4. RIGHT sides of tail piece to body, stitch with ¼" seam around outside edges, leaving extra fabric of tail next to body to tuck inside. Clip curved seam allowances. Turn.

5. Handling both layers of fabric as one, fold on dotted line to make darts in tail. Cut cording length 1" less than dart and place in fold. Stitch dart with zipper foot. Repeat.
6. To attach leg, cut slash and circle; see pattern. RIGHT sides of top of leg and circle together, match edges. Stitch with narrow seam, easing leg piece into circle. RIGHT sides together, stitch leg and slash. Repeat.
7. RIGHT sides of body together, stitch from neck across breast with ¼" seam.
8. RIGHT sides of two foot pieces together, stitch with ¼" seam, leaving opening on one side. Turn; slip stitch opening closed. Repeat.
9. Fold on dotted line; see pattern, matching solid lines. Stitch on solid lines through all layers to make tuck. Press tuck flat; see Diagram 1. Topstitch close to edge around foot piece, keeping tuck flat. Repeat.

Diagram 1

10. Fold ¼" inside at narrow end of leg. Insert narrow end of foot. Stitch securely through all layers by hand or machine.
11. Stuff goose firmly, forcing stuffing into tail one tube at a time with the eraser end of a pencil. Stuff legs very firmly. Slip stitch opening closed.
12. RIGHT sides of heart pieces together, stitch edges, leaving 1" opening. Clip seam allowance at center top. Turn and stuff. Slip stitch opening closed.
13. Fold yellow satin ribbon in half. Tack fold of ribbon securely to back of heart. Tie around goose neck.

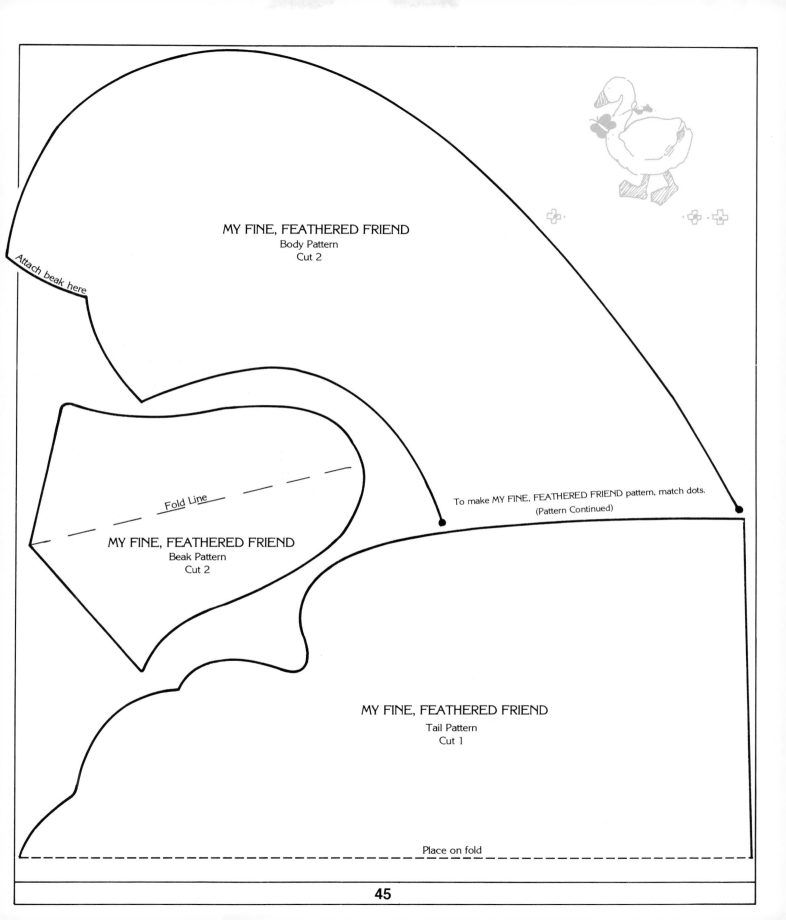

MY FINE, FEATHERED FRIEND
Body Pattern
Cut 2

Attach beak here

Fold Line

MY FINE, FEATHERED FRIEND
Beak Pattern
Cut 2

To make MY FINE, FEATHERED FRIEND pattern, match dots.
(Pattern Continued)

MY FINE, FEATHERED FRIEND

Tail Pattern
Cut 1

Place on fold

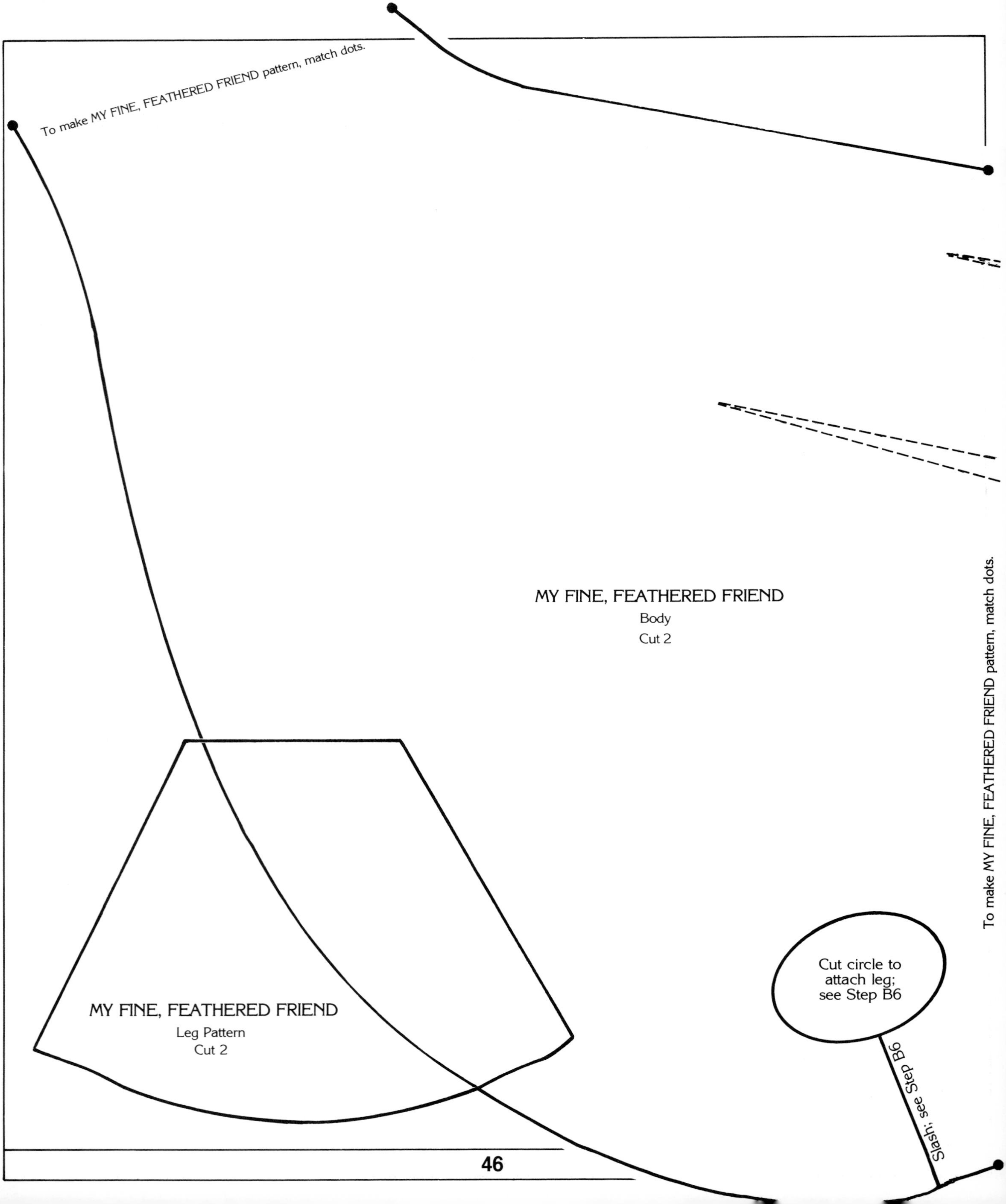

To make MY FINE, FEATHERED FRIEND pattern, match dots.

MY FINE, FEATHERED FRIEND
Body
Cut 2

To make MY FINE, FEATHERED FRIEND pattern, match dots.

MY FINE, FEATHERED FRIEND
Leg Pattern
Cut 2

Cut circle to
attach leg;
see Step B6

Slash; see Step B6

46

My fine, feathered friend

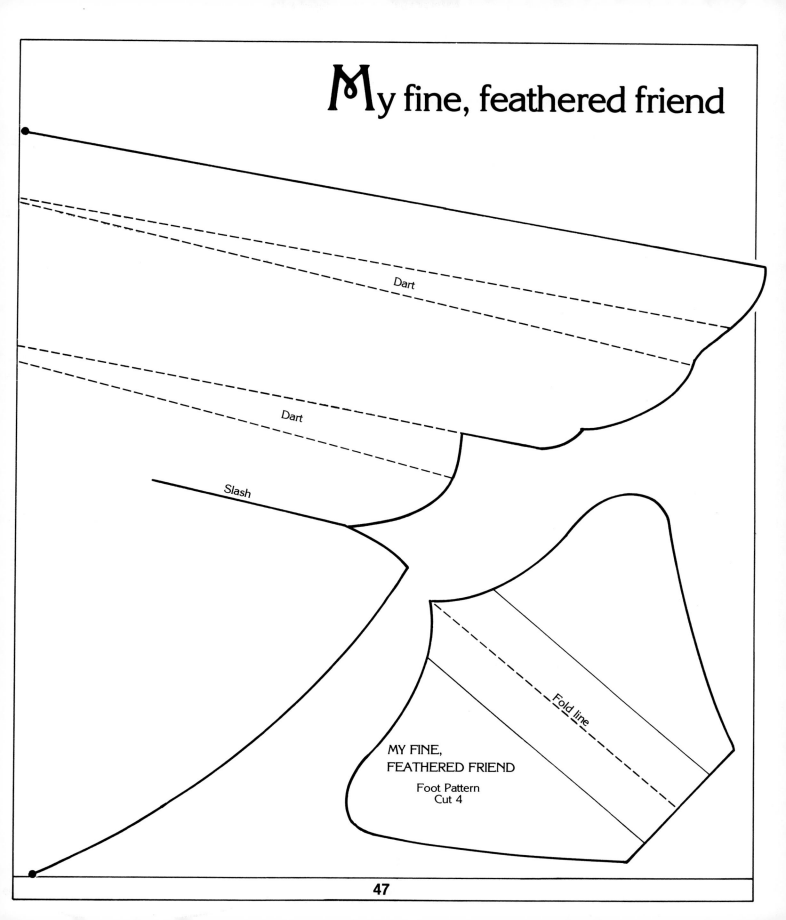

Dart

Dart

Slash

Fold line

MY FINE,
FEATHERED FRIEND

Foot Pattern
Cut 4

Gathering the geese

Stitch Count
78
99

Wee french folk in the village square
Gather the geese from here to there,
Scattering handfuls of meal and corn
To feed them in the early morn.

Poetry by Susan Jeppesen

Gathering the geese

Cover sample: Stitched on Yellow Mono Canvas 22 over two threads. Finished design size is 7" x 8¾". Cut fabric 13" x 15". Finished design sizes using other fabrics are — Aida 11: 7⅛" x 9"; Aida 14: 5⅝" x 7⅛"; Aida 18: 4⅜" x 5½"; Hardanger 22: 3½" x 4½".

Gathering The Geese is cross-stitched on airy, yellow canvas and is a reminder of sunny days spent at Grandma's.

BATES		DMC	(used for cover sample)
		Step One: Cross-stitch (three strands)	
386		746	Off White
306		725	Topaz
323		722	Orange Spice · lt.
778		754	Peach Flesh · lt.
108		211	Lavender · lt.
95		554	Violet · lt.
118		340	Blue Violet · med.
120		794	Cornflower Blue · lt.
121		793	Cornflower Blue · med.
203		564	Jade · vy. lt.
210		562	Jade · med.
882		407	Sportsman Flesh · dk.
397		453	Shell Gray · lt.
399		452	Shell Gray · med.
		Step Two: Back Stitch (one strand)	
210		562	Jade · med. (boy's shirt, lettering)
210		562	Jade · med. (two strands, flower stems)
401		535	Ash Gray · vy. lt. (all else)
		Step Three: French Knots (one strand)	
210		562	Jade · med.
401		535	Ash Gray · vy. lt.
		Step Four: Bead Work	
			Tangerine
			Lilac
			Iris
			Green
			Jade Green

the little french folk

A quilted vest

Materials needed:
⅜ yd. 45" contrasting print fabric for binding
Small pieces of four print fabrics; matching thread
1 yd. ⅜" wide grosgrain ribbon
One 2" x 30" piece batting
Tracing paper for pattern

1. Make simple vest, using purchased pattern and double-faced quilted fabric. Omit all facings.
2. Make triangle pattern on page 51. Divide width of vest by four to determine number of triangles of each color needed. From each of four fabrics, cut triangles.
3. Following Diagram 2 of "The Gosling's Bunting" (page 51), piece triangles in one long strip.
4. Match batting to WRONG side of strip. Pin strip to vest 2" above bottom edge. Turn edges of strip under ¼"; slip stitch. Machine stitch diagonal seams.
5. Stitch grosgrain ribbon ¾" above pieced strip.
6. From fabric for binding, cut 2¼" wide bias strips, piecing as needed, to equal distance around vest and armholes.
7. RIGHT sides together, stitch bias to edge of vest and armholes. Turn bias double to opposite side; slip stitch.

The goslings' bunting

Materials needed:

- 1½ yds. 45" blue with white dot fabric; matching thread
- 1⅛ yds. 45" white with blue dot fabric; matching thread
- ⅜ yd. 45" white seersucker fabric
- ¼ yd. 45" blue print fabric
- ⅛ yd. 45" yellow dot fabric; matching thread
- ⅛ yd. 45" white print fabric
- 1¼ yds. ⅜" wide yellow grosgrain ribbon
- ¼ yd. ⅛" wide yellow grosgrain ribbon
- Fusing material
- Batting
- Small amount of stuffing
- Dressmaker's chalk
- Dressmaker's pen
- Tracing paper for patterns

A. Prepare fabric:
1. Make patterns for goose, goose foot, goose beak, gosling, gosling foot, gosling closed beak, gosling open beak, cloud and triangle. Transfer all information.
2. From white seersucker, cut one goose and three goslings facing right. Cut one gosling facing left. Transfer lines for wing with dressmaker's pen. Also cut twenty triangles.
3. From white with blue dot fabric, cut one 30" x 42" piece for backing. Also cut two 3" x 42" strips for front of bunting.
4. From blue with white dot fabric, cut one 12½" x 42" strip for center panel of front, two 3¾" x 42" strips for front, and one 3" x 45" strip for tie. For binding, cut 2½" wide bias strips, piecing as needed, to equal 3 yds.
5. From yellow dot fabric, cut twenty triangles, two goose foot pieces, eight gosling foot pieces, one goose beak piece, three gosling closed beak pieces and one gosling open beak piece.
6. From blue print fabric, cut one 2½" x 42" strip and twenty triangles.
7. From white print fabric, cut twenty triangles.
8. From fusing material, cut goose and gosling pieces, omitting wing section. Also cut all beak and foot pieces.

B. Construct bunting front:
1. Pin fusing material pieces to WRONG sides of goose and gosling pieces. Position pieces on center panel according to Diagram 1.
2. Fuse pieces according to manufacturer's instructions, leaving wing area of each body unattached.

3. Using white thread and medium width satin stitch, machine applique all body pieces, stitching interior wing lines first. Insert small amount of stuffing under wing areas and satin stitch outside body lines.
4. Using yellow thread and narrow satin stitch, machine applique around beaks, feet and legs.
5. Using blue thread and narrow satin stitch, sew eyes.
6. Piece together triangles to make two 43" long strips with pattern which repeats every fourth piece; see Diagram 2.
7. RIGHT sides together and using ¼" seam, stitch one 3¾" x 42" blue with white dot fabric strip to one 3" x 42" white with blue dot fabric strip. Stitch one pieced strip to second edge of white with blue dot fabric strip.
8. Continue to piece front by stitching strips together. Attach blue print strip to second long edge of pieced strip, then center panel, second pieced strip, white with blue dot strip and blue with white dot strip.
9. Cut ⅛" wide yellow grosgrain ribbon into two equal lengths. Pin lengths to either side of goose neck; see pattern. Tack ends securely and tie into bow.

C. Complete bunting:
1. Place white with blue dot fabric WRONG side up on flat surface. Center batting and bunting front over backing. Baste thoroughly.
2. Using white thread, quilt by hand around goose and gosling bodies. Quilt on all horizontal seam lines. Also quilt horizontal lines shown in Diagram 1.
3. Trace cloud pattern with dressmaker's pen on bunting following Diagram 1. Quilt on pen lines to make five clouds.
4. Cut ⅜" wide grosgrain ribbon into four equal lengths for ties. Pin with raw edges matching, 10" and 20" from top edge of bunting; see Diagram 1.
5. RIGHT sides of bias strip and bunting front together, stitch through all layers with ½" seam around sides and top, securing ribbon ties in seam and allowing some additional fullness in bias at corners. Fold bias double to lining and slip stitch.
6. To make casing, fold 2" at each end of remaining bias strip to WRONG side. RIGHT sides of bias and bottom edge of bunting front together, stitch with ½" seam. Fold bias double to lining and slip stitch securely, leaving ends open.
7. RIGHT sides of tie strip together, stitch with ½" seam. Turn. Knot each end. Thread through casing. To keep tie from pulling out, tack tie through all layers at center back of bunting. Bunting may be folded and tied or used flat as a quilt.

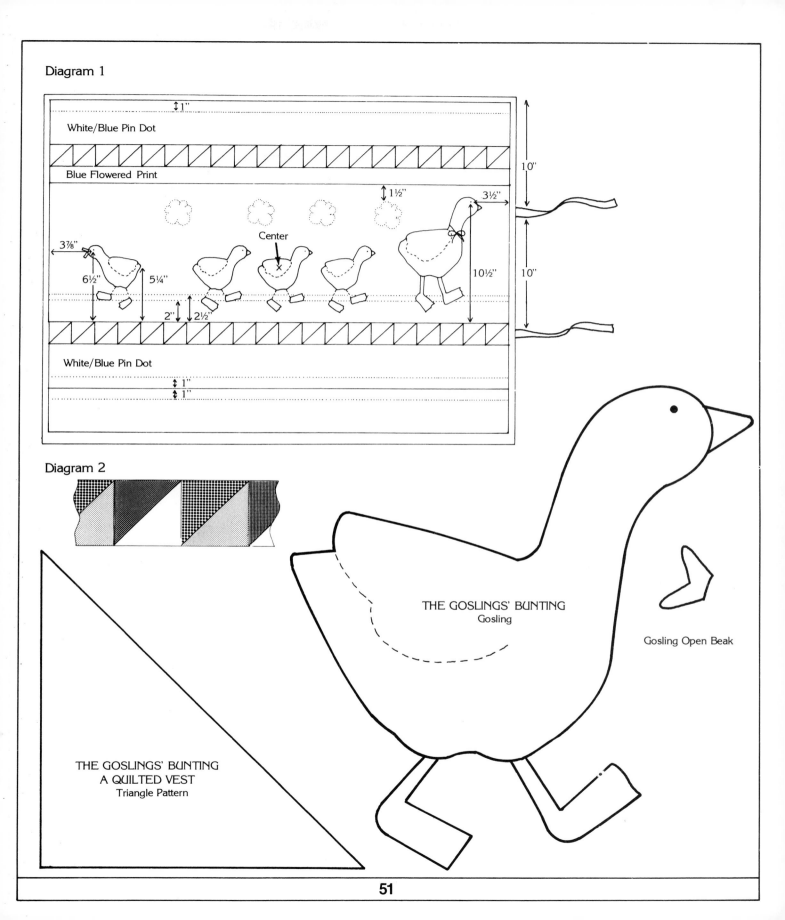

Diagram 1

White/Blue Pin Dot

↕ 1"

Blue Flowered Print

1½"

3½"

3⅞"

Center

6½"   5¼"

10½"

2"   2½"

White/Blue Pin Dot

↕ 1"
↕ 1"

10"

10"

Diagram 2

THE GOSLINGS' BUNTING
A QUILTED VEST
Triangle Pattern

THE GOSLINGS' BUNTING
Gosling

Gosling Open Beak

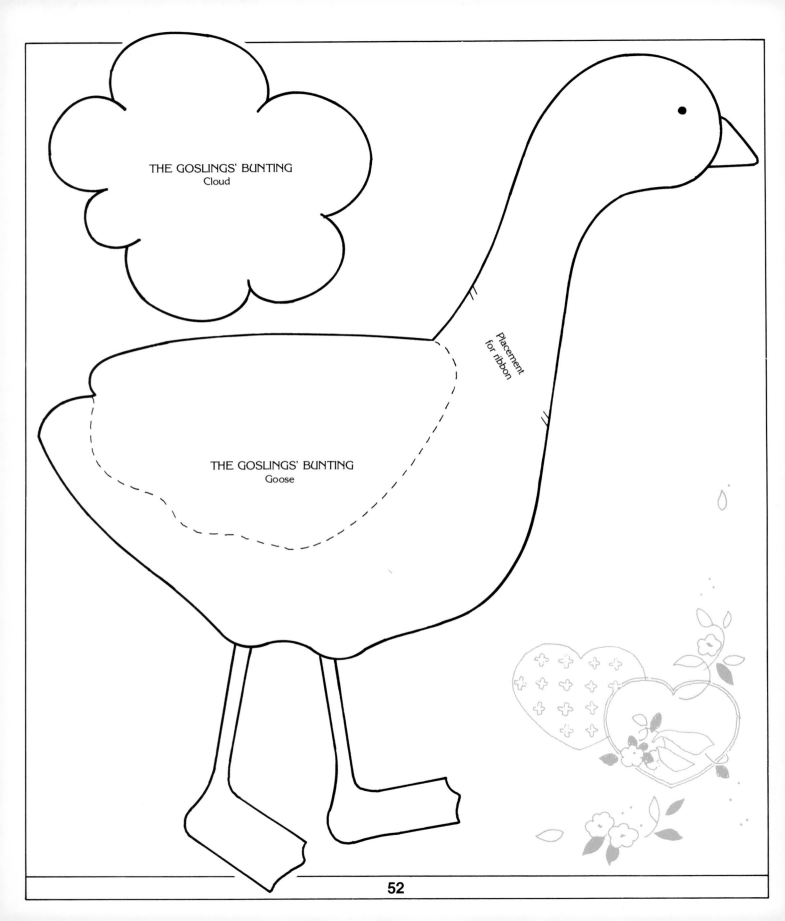

THE GOSLINGS' BUNTING
Cloud

Placement for ribbon

THE GOSLINGS' BUNTING
Goose

A stenciled notebook

Materials needed:
   One blue canvas notebook larger than 8½" x 8½" design
   Blue, yellow and white paints
   Stenciling materials; see Stenciling Instructions
   Option: Scotchguard

1. Make stencils for goose. To make stencil for border, draw 8½" x 8½" square. Draw parallel lines ½" inside first lines. Divide border into ½" square blocks; see pattern.

2. Stencil border with blue paint. Stencil goose with white paint, then beak and feet with yellow paint. Allow paint to dry thoroughly between applications.

3. Option: Waterproof notebook with Scotchguard.

April

April's child, like a lamb soft and fair,
With wondering eyes and curling hair,
Sleeps with a quilt sewn in ribbon hues
And knows with the morn that dreams come true.

Cuddling up with this soft Puffed Lamb, sleep comes easily.

Opposite page: Sweet Dreams, cross-stitched in pastel colors, watches over a child who is counting sheep. The Lamb Pillow, An Eyelet Pillow and The Pastel Ribbon Pillow will become bedtime friends. With one arm around the Puffed Lamb and his head on For A Baby's Nap, a child's bedtime will be the nicest time of the day.

Sleep under a warm quilt
and all your dreams will come true.

Sweet dreams

Cover sample: Stitched on White Linda 27 over two threads. Finished design size is 7" x 8¼". Cut fabric 13" x 15". Finished design sizes using other fabrics are — Aida 11: 8⅝" x 10⅛"; Aida 14: 6¾" x 8"; Aida 18: 5¼" x 6¼"; Hardanger 22: 4⅜" x 5⅛".

BATES		DMC	(used for cover sample)
			Step One: Cross-stitch (two strands)
1			White
292		3078	Golden Yellow · vy. lt.
297		743	Yellow · med.
880		948	Peach Flesh · vy. lt.
778		754	Peach Flesh · lt.
35		3326	Rose · lt.
894		223	Shell Pink · med.
108		211	Lavender · lt.
99		552	Violet · dk.
118		340	Blue Violet · med.
128		800	Delft · pale
130		799	Delft · med.
121		793	Cornflower Blue · med.
940		792	Cornflower Blue · dk.
206		955	Nile Green · lt.
187		992	Aquamarine
5975		356	Terra Cotta · med.
371		433	Brown · med.
378		841	Beige Brown · lt.
			Step Two: Back Stitch (one strand)
905		645	Beaver Gray · vy. dk.
			Step Three: French Knots (one strand)
905		645	Beaver Gray · vy. dk.

Puffed lamb

Materials needed:
½ yd. white single knit fabric; matching thread
¼ yd. blue single knit fabric; matching thread
¼ yd. muslin
Two ¼" wide black buttons
Small cow bell
1 yd. 1½" wide plaid ribbon
Polyester fleece
Stuffing
Tracing paper and cardboard for patterns

A. Prepare fabric:
1. From tracing paper, make patterns for head, gusset and ear. Also make 3¼" and 3" wide circle patterns; see General Instructions.
2. From cardboard, make patterns for 2¼" x 2¼" pieces, 3" x 3" pieces and 2¾" wide circles.
3. From white knit, cut two ear pieces, sixty-six 3" x 3" pieces, two 3" wide circles and twenty-seven 2¾" wide circles.
4. From blue knit, cut two ear pieces, two head pieces and one gusset piece. Also cut four 3¼" circles and four 3⅝" x 6" strips for legs.
5. From muslin, cut sixty-six 2¼" x 2¼" pieces.
6. From fleece, cut two ear pieces. Trim ¼" from all edges.

B. Construct lamb:
1. To make each block, place WRONG sides of one piece of white and one piece of muslin together, matching corners; pin. Fold excess white fabric into tuck in center of each edge and pin; see Diagram 1. Stitch ¼" from edge around entire block through both layers. Repeat for remaining sixty-six blocks.

Diagram 1

2. RIGHT sides of white fabric together, join blocks with ½" seams to make six rows of eleven blocks each. RIGHT sides of rows together, join rows with ½" seams.

(Continued)

3. To stuff blocks, work from WRONG side and carefully make 1½" diagonal slit in muslin only. Stuff moderately. Slip stitch openings closed. Repeat for each block; see Diagram 2.

Diagram 2

4. RIGHT sides together, stitch six-block sides to form cylinder. Stitch gathering thread around both ends of cylinder. Gather one end to make opening 1" wide; secure threads.
5. By hand, stitch gathering thread around 3" wide circles. Gather both slightly and stuff firmly; secure threads. Place one circle over gathered opening at end of cylinder; slip stitch securely to seam allowance of blocks. Stuff cylinder firmly. Attach second stuffed 3" circle to second end.
6. To make head, stitch head pieces to gusset with ¼" seam matching A's and B's on pattern. By hand, shape head as shown in photo. Turn under ¼" around neck and baste. Stuff. Place on one end of cylinder, covering two puffs, and slip stitch securely; see photo.

7. RIGHT sides of one white ear and one blue ear together, stitch with ¼" seam, leaving opening as indicated on pattern; turn. Place fleece inside ear next to seam. Topstitch ear ¼" from edge. Repeat for second ear. Place ears on head ½" below seam line; see photo. Slip stitch securely.
8. By hand, stitch gathering thread ¼" from edge of twenty-seven 2¾" wide circles. Gather slightly and stuff. Gather tightly and secure thread. Slip stitch circles to head and neck as shown in photo.
9. To sew on buttons for eyes, bring double strand of white thread in at neck line and through head at seam line at least two times for each button, indenting eyes slightly. Secure thread at neck.
10. To make legs, fold blue strips with RIGHT sides together and stitch 3⅝" sides to form circle. RIGHT sides together, stitch one edge of strip to 3¼" circle with ¼" seam. Turn; stuff. Slip stitch securely to lamb's body with two rows of blocks between right and left legs and three rows of blocks between front and back legs. Seam of legs should be toward center bottom of lamb.
11. To make hooves, use blue thread and take three ¼" deep stitches through circle and front of each leg; pull tightly and secure.
12. Tie ribbon around lamb's neck with bell in bow. Trim ends diagonally.

A

PUFFED LAMB
Gusset

Cut 1

To make PUFFED LAMB pattern, match dots.
(Pattern continued)

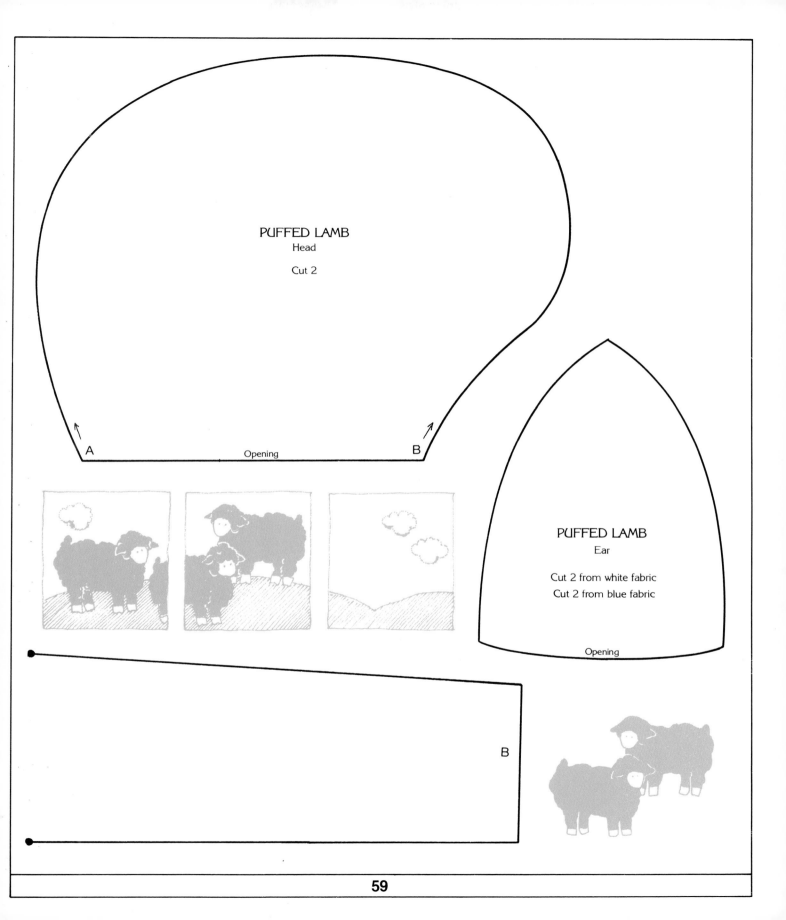

PUFFED LAMB
Head

Cut 2

A

Opening

B

PUFFED LAMB
Ear

Cut 2 from white fabric
Cut 2 from blue fabric

Opening

B

For a baby's nap

Materials needed:
5¼ yds. 45" lightweight apricot fabric; matching thread
1½ yds. 45" apricot print fabric
10 yds. ⅛" wide apricot satin ribbon
12 yds. medium cording
Batting
Large-eyed needle
Dressmaker's pen
Safety pins

A. Prepare fabric:
  1. From apricot fabric, cut one 45" x 49" piece for back and ten 5" x 66" pieces for front.
  2. From print, cut 2" wide bias strips, piecing as needed, to equal nine 3 yd. strips.
  3. From batting, cut one 45" x 48" piece.
B. Construct quilt:
  1. Mark both long sides of each strip of apricot fabric with dressmaker's pen as shown in Diagram 1.

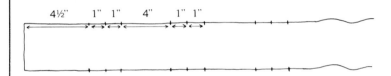

  2. Pin pleats ½" deep on each side of mark in center of 1" segments; press. See Diagram 2.

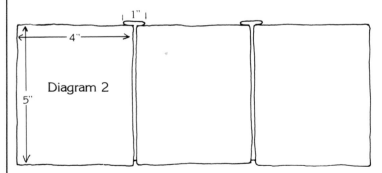

Diagram 2

  3. To make cording, stitch gathering threads on both edges of bias strips. Pulling all four rows of stitching at once, gather each 3 yd. strip to 46".
  4. Cut cording into nine 46" pieces. Place cording in center of WRONG side of gathered bias. Fold bias over cording and stitch with zipper foot close to cording. Repeat for eight additional strips.

5. Place cording on long right edge of RIGHT side of apricot strip, raw edges matching. Stitch with ½" seam. Repeat for eight additional strips. Trim seam allowance of all cording to ¼".
6. RIGHT side of two strips together, stitch with cording in seam. Continue to join strips, adding strip without cording last. Open out top. It should measure 41" x 45".
7. Press and baste all seam allowances the same direction.
8. Place quilt back WRONG side up on flat surface. Cover with batting. Center quilt top over both layers. Pin at frequent intervals with safety pins, keeping back smooth.
9. With matching thread, quilt through center (between folds) of each pleat; see Diagram 4. Also stitch small gathering thread through top layer of pleat only; see Diagram 3. Gather slightly and secure through all layers, see Diagram 4.

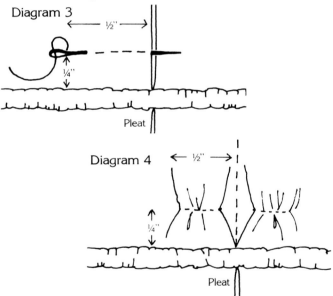

Diagram 3

Diagram 4

10. Wrap edge of quilt batting and back to front, folding ¼" seam allowance under and overlapping front edge ½". Slip stitch to quilt front. At corners, trim excess fabric and ease fullness, tacking as needed to control fullness.
11. With matching thread, quilt around entire quilt near seam joining back to front.
12. Mark placement for ribbon on every other pleat of every other row over cording; see photo. Cut ribbon into twenty-five 14" pieces. Thread ribbon into large-eyed needle and stitch through all layers, working from top to back and to top again. Tie into bow. Tie knots ½" from both ends.

An eyelet pillow

Materials needed:
   ⅜ yd. white fabric; matching thread
   3¾ yds. ¼" wide white satin ribbon
   1¼ yds. 6" wide flat white eyelet
   One 14" x 14" knife edge pillow form
   Dressmaker's pen

1. From white fabric, cut two 13" x 13" pieces.
2. Cut eyelet into three 13" pieces. Place first piece with finished edge 2" from right edge of one 13" x 13" fabric piece. Stitch left edge of eyelet to pillow top. Place second piece of eyelet with finished edge 5" from right edge of fabric piece and overlapping first eyelet; stitch. Place third piece of eyelet with finished edge 8" from right edge of fabric piece and stitch to left edge of fabric; trim excess eyelet.
3. With dressmaker's pen, mark vertical lines 4¼", 7¼" and 10" from right edge of pillow. On each line, mark 1" intervals.
4. Cut three 26" lengths of ribbon. With dressmaker's pen, mark ribbon at 2" intervals.
5. Matching edge of ribbon to top edge of pillow top, tack one ribbon length to top of each line. Stitch each mark on ribbons to 1" marks on pillow top. Tack each ribbon loop ½" right of vertical lines; see Diagram 1.
6. RIGHT sides of pillow top and remaining white fabric piece together, stitch with ½" seam, leaving 8" opening. Clip corners and turn. Insert pillow form and slip stitch opening closed.
7. Cut three 18" lengths from remaining ribbon. Tie 4" wide bow with each piece and knot ends. Tack bows to bottom of each ribbon. Remove pen marks.

Diagram 1

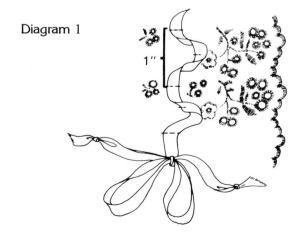

Pastel ribbon pillow

Materials needed:
   1½ yds. 45" lightweight fabric; matching thread
   5 yds. ⅛" wide ribbon; matching thread
   One 11" x 11" knife edge pillow form

A. Prepare fabric:
  1. From fabric, cut 8" wide bias strips, piecing as needed to equal 4½ yds. Fold with RIGHT sides together and join ends to make one continuous piece. Also cut one 10" x 10" piece for pillow back.
B. Construct pillow:
  1. Stitch gathering threads on one edge of bias piece. Gather tightly to about 12".
  2. Fold bias with RIGHT sides together, matching gathered edges; stitch with ½" seam. Force gathering into seam as needed to make seam 6" long. Trim seam allowance to ¼". Remove only gathering threads which show on RIGHT side.
  3. Place bias pillow top RIGHT side up on flat surface. Fold pillow back diagonally and crease fold. Place crease line over seam in bias with RIGHT sides together; pin. Dispersing gathers evenly along outside edge of pillow back, baste both layers together. Trim excess bias. Stitch with ½" seam, using edge of pillow back as guide and rounding off corners slightly; leave 5" opening. Turn.
  4. From ribbon, cut one 2½ yd. length. Secure thread in one end of ribbon and take small stitch at 1½" intervals, gathering ribbon while stitching; see Diagram 1. Gather ribbon to 4½". Tack ribbon to seam of pillow top; see photo.
  5. Insert pillow form. Slip stitch opening closed.
  6. From remaining ribbon, cut six 12" pieces. Handling three pieces as one, tie into bow and tack securely at end of gathered ribbon. Repeat for second end.

Diagram 1

Lamb pillow

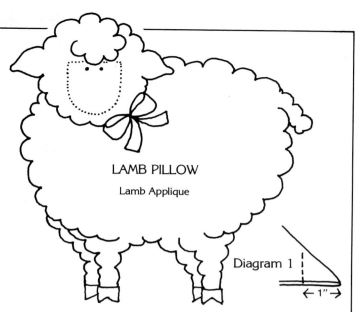

LAMB PILLOW

Lamb Applique

Diagram 1

← 1" →

Materials needed:

2⅜ yds. 45" lightweight blue print fabric; matching thread
7½" x 7½" piece solid color fabric; matching thread
Two small pieces white seersucker
17 dozen blue sew-on beads
Three apricot sew-on beads
Apricot thread
Fusing material
Embroidery floss in two shades of apricot and two shades of blue
One 12" x 12" box pillow form
Dressmaker's pen
Tracing paper for patterns

A. Prepare fabric:
1. Make patterns for lamb and lamb face, adding ⅛" seam allowance. Also make 7½" circle patterns; see General Instructions.
2. From print fabric, cut two 15" x 15" pieces and 6" wide bias strips, piecing as needed, to equal 6¾ yds. Also cut 4" wide bias strips, piecing as needed, to equal 3 yds.
3. From solid color fabric, cut one 7½" circle and three lamb's faces.
4. On seersucker, trace one lamb with head on left side; cut out. Reverse pattern and trace second lamb with head on right. Reposition pattern over second lamb (see photo) and trace third lamb. Cut second and third lamb as one piece.
5. From fusing material, cut one 7½" circle and pieces to match lamb bodies.

B. Construct pillow:
1. Center circle on RIGHT side of one 15" x 15" piece with fusing material between fabrics; fuse according to manufacturer's instructions. With matching thread and wide satin stitch, machine applique entire edge of circle.
2. Position lambs (see photo) with fusing material between fabrics; fuse. Position lamb faces. Turn raw edges under ⅛" and slip stitch.
3. With dressmaker's pen, draw detail lines and bows on lambs. With apricot thread and narrow satin stitch, machine embroider lamb's fleece on each lamb.
4. By hand, satin stitch all hooves in darker apricot floss.
5. By hand, satin stitch bow on right lamb using apricot

thread and lighter apricot floss. Satin stitch bows on both left lambs in two shades of blue.
6. With one strand dark blue floss, make French knots for lamb's eyes, wrapping floss twice around needle.
7. Draw circles with dressmaker's pen 1" outside edge of fabric circle and 1¼" inside edge of fabric circle between lambs. Attach blue beads ⅛" apart over entire edge of fabric circle over satin stitch and over inside circle; see photo. Also attach three blue beads in center of each blue bow and three apricot beads in center of apricot bow.
8. RIGHT sides together, join ends of 6" wide bias strips to make one continuous piece. Stitch gathering threads along one raw edge. Gather to about 30". RIGHT sides together, place gathered edge on largest circle (drawn with dressmaker's pen) and stitch bias ½" from edge.
9. Fold bias RIGHT side out and baste to edges of pillow top, dispersing fullness evenly. Trim bias to fit pillow top.
10. In each corner of pillow top and pillow back, pin 1" deep tucks; see Diagram 1.
11. RIGHT sides together, join ends of 4" wide bias to make one continuous piece. WRONG sides together, fold to measure 2" wide and press fold line. Fold bias into four equal lengths and mark quarters. Stitch gathering threads along raw edges through both layers. Match quarter marks to corners of pillow top. Gather bias to fit and, RIGHT sides together, stitch with ½" seam.
12. RIGHT sides of pillow top and pillow back together, match corners with ruffle folded toward center. Stitch top and back together with ½" seam, keeping ruffle smooth and leaving 8" opening. Turn. Insert pillow form. Slip stitch opening closed.

Opposite page: Lasting long after a favorite blanket is worn out, Sweet Dreams reminds a child of his mother's loving touch. Each of the pillows - the Lamb Pillow, An Eyelet Pillow and the Pastel Ribbon Pillow - can be made from a favorite fabric in favorite colors.

May

May's child is sent from the angels above
With white satin ribbons and tended with love.
Hearts and rainbows and doves of blue
Carry my wishes and hopes for you.

A Child's Sampler, stitched in such a wide range of soft colors, will fit the decor of a child's room for years.

Opposite page: The walls of this room sing with the cheerful spring colors of The Rainbow Wallhanging, Birds-On-The-Wing, a garland, and A Child's Sampler. Joining the chorus are the tiny birds on The Sunsuit and the pink Hanger and Sachet. Harmonizing with the theme are the Yellow Ruffled Pillow, the White Shirred Pillow and The Rainbow Quilt on the bed. Only the music of a child is needed to complete this setting.

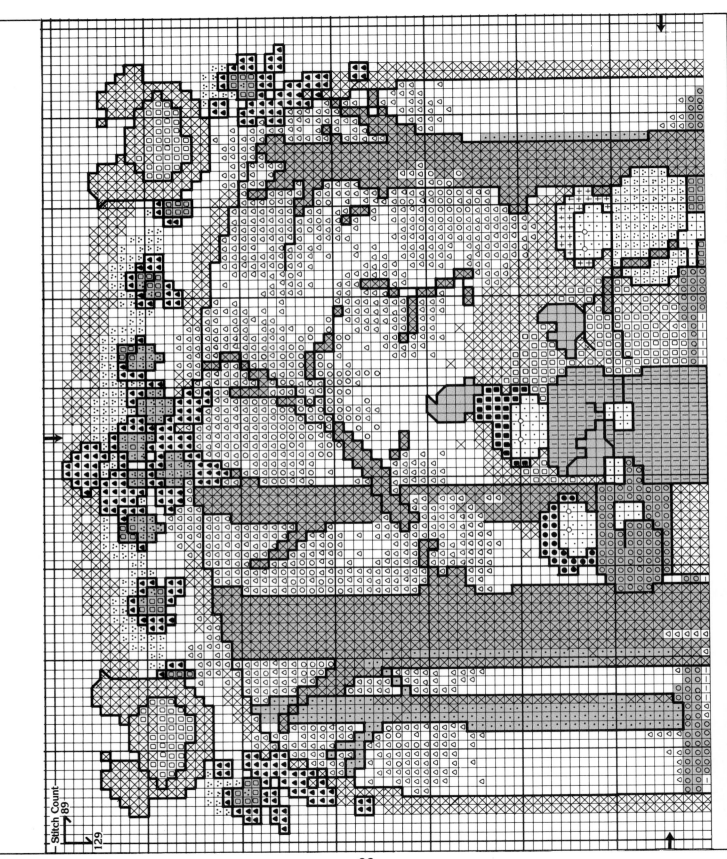

Stitch Count
89
129

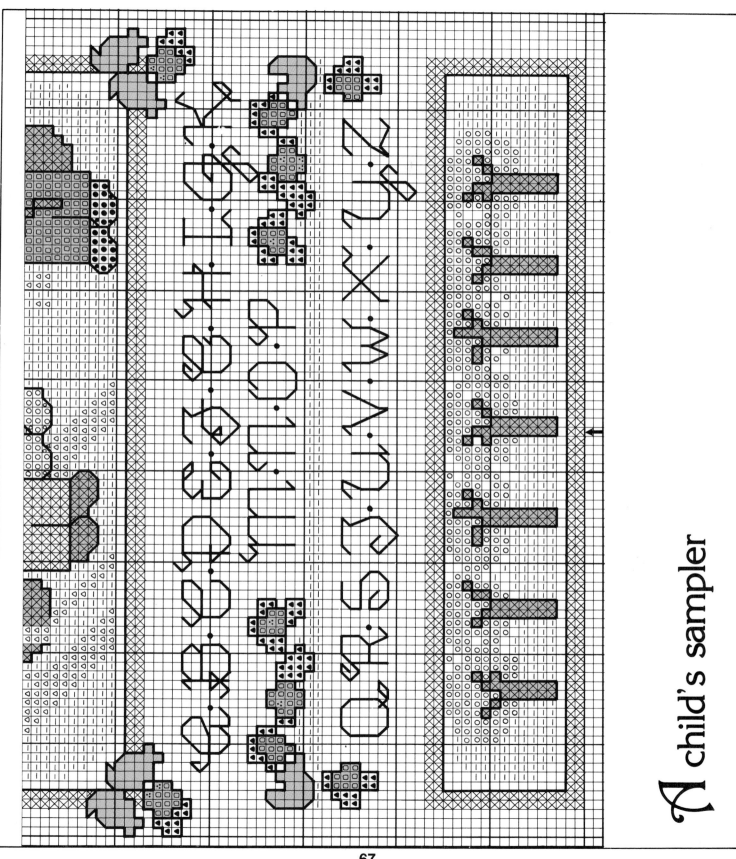

A child's sampler

A child's sampler

Cover sample: Stitched on Yellow Hardanger 22 over two threads. Finished design size is 8⅛" x 11¾". Cut fabric 14" x 18". Finished design sizes using other fabrics are — Aida 11: 8⅛" x 11¾"; Aida 14: 6⅜" x 9¼"; Aida 18: 5" x 7⅛"; Hardanger 22: 4" x 5⅞".

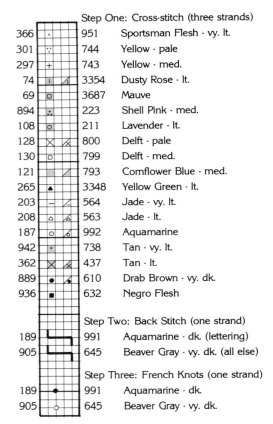

BATES		DMC	(used for cover sample)
			Step One: Cross-stitch (three strands)
366		951	Sportsman Flesh · vy. lt.
301		744	Yellow · pale
297		743	Yellow · med.
74		3354	Dusty Rose · lt.
69		3687	Mauve
894		223	Shell Pink · med.
108		211	Lavender · lt.
128		800	Delft · pale
130		799	Delft · med.
121		793	Cornflower Blue · med.
265		3348	Yellow Green · lt.
203		564	Jade · vy. lt.
208		563	Jade · lt.
187		992	Aquamarine
942		738	Tan · vy. lt.
362		437	Tan · lt.
889		610	Drab Brown · vy. dk.
936		632	Negro Flesh
			Step Two: Back Stitch (one strand)
189		991	Aquamarine · dk. (lettering)
905		645	Beaver Gray · vy. dk. (all else)
			Step Three: French Knots (one strand)
189		991	Aquamarine · dk.
905		645	Beaver Gray · vy. dk.

YELLOW RUFFLED PILLOW DIAGRAMS

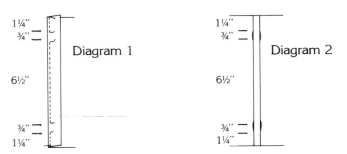

1¼"
¾"

Diagram 1

6½"

¾"
1¼"

1¼"
¾"

Diagram 2

6½"

¾"
1¼"

Yellow ruffled pillow

Materials needed:
1½ yds. 45" yellow fabric; matching thread
⅛ yd. 45" print fabric
1½ yds. 1" wide white satin ribbon; matching thread
10½" x 14½" piece batting
Stuffing
Safety pins

A. Prepare fabric:
  1. From yellow fabric, cut two 10½" x 14½" pieces and six 2¼" x 10½" pieces. Also cut 10" wide bias strips, piecing as needed, to equal 3 yds.
  2. From print fabric, cut seven 1" x 10½" strips.
B. Construct pillow:
  1. To piece pillow top, place RIGHT sides of one yellow strip and one print strip together. Stitch with ¼" seam, leaving openings, as shown in Diagram 1; back stitch. Continue to stitch together alternating strips, leaving openings; see Diagram 2. Press all seam allowances under print strips.
  2. Place one 10½" x 14½" piece on flat surface and cover with batting. Center pillow top, RIGHT side up, over batting; baste together. Stitch through all layers with yellow thread on yellow strips very close to seams.
  3. Cut two 15" lengths of ribbon. Thread under print strips through openings on pillow top. Slip stitch fullness in ribbon to print strips without pulling ribbon tightly between strips.
  4. RIGHT sides of 10" ends of bias together, stitch with ¼" seam. Fold WRONG sides together to measure 5"; press. Divide bias into quarters and mark on raw edge with safety pins. Stitch gathering threads on raw edge. Also mark centers of each edge of pillow top.
  5. RIGHT sides of pillow top and bias together, match raw edges and marks; pin. Gather bias to match edges; stitch with ¼" seam.
  6. RIGHT sides of pillow top and back together, stitch on stitching line for ruffle, leaving 8" opening in bottom edge. Clip corners; turn. Stuff pillow firmly; slip stitch opening closed.
  7. Tie remaining ribbon into 6" wide bow and tack to next to last strip on lower right side of pillow top; see photo.

Birds on-the-wing

GARLAND

Materials needed:
¼ yd. 45" print fabric; matching thread
⅛ yd. 45" white fabric; matching thread
Small pieces yellow fabric; matching thread
4½ yds. ⅛" wide satin ribbon
Black embroidery floss
Stuffing
Tracing paper for patterns

A. Prepare fabric:
   1. Make patterns for bird body, wing and gusset, transferring all information. Also make pattern for heart.
   2. From print fabric, cut pieces needed for three birds. From white fabric, cut pieces for two birds. From yellow fabric, cut pieces for three hearts.
B. Construct toy:
   1. RIGHT sides of bird gusset and one body piece together, stitch between marks on pattern with ¼" seam. Repeat for second body piece with stitching meeting first seam.
   2. RIGHT sides of body together, stitch from both ends of gusset to opening in center back (see pattern); back stitch. Turn, stuff and slip stitch opening closed.
   3. RIGHT sides of two wing pieces together, stitch with ¼" seam, leaving 1" opening at top of wing. Turn, stuff and slip stitch opening closed. Repeat with remaining wing pieces.
   4. With matching thread, quilt by hand where indicated on wing and body patterns. Place wings on body and tack at shoulder of wing.
   5. With one strand black embroidery floss, make French knots for eyes, wrapping floss around needle twice.
   6. Fold ribbon in half. Tack fold to center back seam of bird's neck. Tie small bow around neck and tack to body. Knot ends of ribbon and trim ¼" from knots.
   7. RIGHT sides together, stitch hearts with ¼" seam, leaving 1" opening. Turn; stuff; slip stitch opening closed.
   8. Complete five birds and three hearts. Tack together as desired; see photo.
   9. Cut two 1 yd. lengths of ribbon. Fold in half. Tack fold to ends of garland.

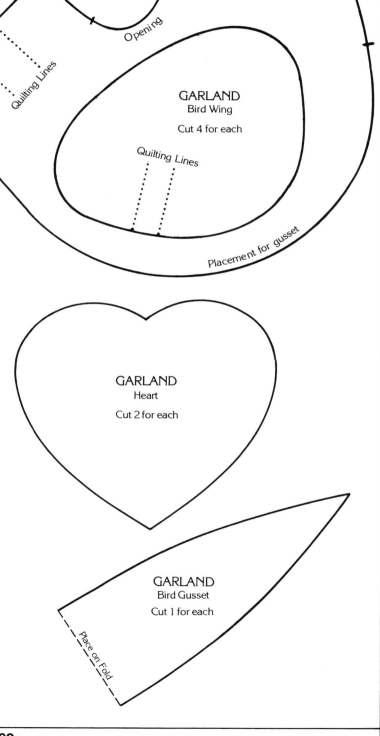

GARLAND
Bird Body
Cut 2 for each

Opening

Quilting Lines

GARLAND
Bird Wing
Cut 4 for each

Quilting Lines

Placement for gusset

GARLAND
Heart
Cut 2 for each

GARLAND
Bird Gusset
Cut 1 for each

Place on Fold

White shirred pillow

Materials needed:
2½ yds. 45" lightweight white fabric; matching thread
¼ yd. 45" white eyelet
5¼ yds. ¾" wide white flat trim
1 yd. ⅝" wide contrasting satin ribbon; matching thread
Stuffing
Safety pins

A. Prepare fabric:
1. From lightweight fabric, cut two 4½" x 20" pieces for shirred ends and two 9" x 13" pieces for lining. Also cut 5" wide bias strips, piecing as needed, to equal two 3½ yd. pieces.
2. From eyelet fabric, cut one 9" x 13" piece for back and one 5" x 9" piece for center front.

B. Construct pillow:
1. Stitch gathering threads on both 20" edges of both pieces for shirring. Gather all edges to 9".
2. Match centers of 5" edges of eyelet and centers of 13" edges of one lining piece; pin together. RIGHT sides together, stitch one gathered edge of each shirred piece to one 9" edge of eyelet with ¼" seam, stitching through lining. Fold shirred piece with WRONG side to lining and match second gathered edge to 9" edge of lining; stitch ¼" from raw edges. Repeat for second end of eyelet with second shirred piece.
3. Cut four 9" lengths of trim. Disperse gathers evenly in shirring and mark vertical center. Stitch raw edge of one piece of trim to center. Turn under ⅛" and stitch second piece over raw edge of first. Repeat for second piece of shirring.
4. Cut one 9" length of ribbon. Fold in half and slip stitch to pillow top over inside seam of left shirring.
5. RIGHT sides of 5" ends of each bias strip together, stitch with ¼" seam to make two continuous pieces. RIGHT sides of one bias strip and trim together, match raw edges and stitch with ¼" seam. RIGHT sides of both bias strips together, match end seams and stitch together on stitching line for trim. Turn and press.
6. Divide raw edge of bias strip into quarters; mark with safety pins. Stitch gathering thread along raw edge. Also mark centers of each edge of pillow top.
7. RIGHT sides of pillow top and bias together, match raw edges and marks. Gather bias to match edges. Stitch ruffle to pillow top with ¼" seam.
8. Pin lining to WRONG side of eyelet back. RIGHT sides of back and front together, stitch on stitching line of ruffle, leaving 6" opening in bottom edge. Turn. Stuff pillow firmly; slip stitch opening closed.
9. Cut remaining ribbon into two equal lengths. Tie into 3" wide bows and tack at each end of ribbon on pillow front.

Hanger and sachet

Materials needed:
One plastic hanger
⅜ yd. 45" fabric; matching thread
½ yd. ⅜" wide lace
Polyester fleece
Stuffing
Potpourri
Tracing paper for patterns

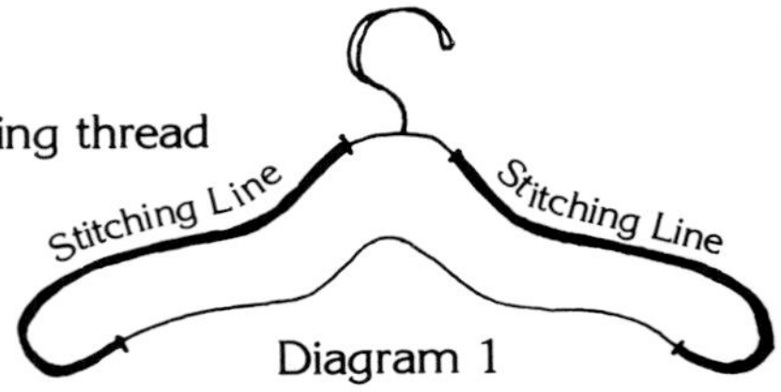

Stitching Line   Stitching Line

Diagram 1

1. To make pattern, trace outline of plastic hanger, omitting hook. Add ¾" seam allowance to entire outside edge. Also make heart pattern.
2. From fabric, cut two pieces like hanger pattern. Also cut two heart pieces and one 1½" x 26" strip for gusset.
3. From fleece, cut two pieces like hanger pattern.
4. Pin fleece to WRONG sides of hanger pieces. RIGHT sides together, stitch with ¼" seam as indicated in Diagram 1. Trim fleece from seam allowance. Clip curved seam allowances; turn.
5. Place hanger between layers of fleece, exposing hook. Fold inside ¼" at top opening and slip stitch securely close to hanger neck.
6. Beginning at one end of large opening, add small amounts of stuffing to pad hanger. Slip stitch several inches, pad more of hanger and slip stitch again. Continue until hanger is evenly padded about ½" thick and entire bottom edge is closed.
7. RIGHT sides of 1½" ends of gusset together, stitch with ¼" seam to make one continuous piece. Stitch gathering threads on both edges of gusset.
8. RIGHT sides together, match seam of gusset to top center of one heart piece. Gather gusset to fit heart, allowing slightly more fullness at bottom; stitch. Repeat, leaving 3" opening.
9. Fill with stuffing and potpourri. Slip stitch opening closed. Attach ends of lace to top of heart back. Hang sachet over hanger.

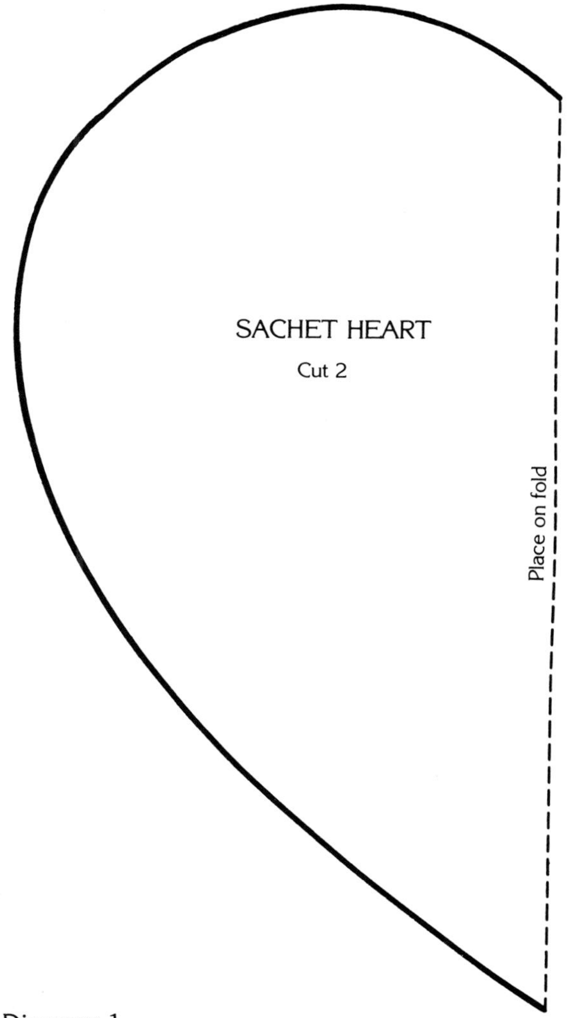

SACHET HEART

Cut 2

Place on fold

Diagram 1

Green
Blue
Yellow
Blue

Green | Green

Pink
Green
Yellow
Green

The rainbow wallhanging

Materials needed:
    1¼ yds. 45" yellow fabric; matching thread
    ⅝ yd. 45" green fabric; matching thread
    ⅝ yd. 45" blue fabric
    ⅛ yd. 45" pink fabric; matching thread
    Small pieces yellow print, pink print, white with pink dot,
        and lavender fabrics for applique
    2⅜ yds. ⅛" wide blue dot satin ribbon
    1⅞ yds. ⅛" wide yellow satin ribbon
    1¼ yds. ⅛" wide pink satin ribbon
    ½ yd. ⅛" wide green satin ribbon
    Bright blue thread
    Fusing material
    Batting
    One 40" length ½" dowel
    Dressmaker's pen
    Tracing paper for patterns

A. Prepare fabric:
    1. Make patterns for applique.
    2. From yellow fabric, cut one 41½" x 33½" piece for
       back, two 2½" x 35½" strips and three 2" x 4" for
       loops. Also cut two rainbow pieces for applique.
    3. From green fabric, cut two 3½" x 45" and two 3½" x
       37" strips for border and one 2½" x 35½" strip. Also
       cut three stems and three sets of leaves.
    4. From blue fabric, cut one 35½" x 17½" piece and one
       2½" x 35½" strip.
    5. From pink fabric, cut one 2½" x 35½" strip. Also cut
       three wide bands for pot.
    6. From yellow print fabric, cut three pots. From pink
       print fabric, cut three hearts.
    7. From white with pink dot fabric, cut three "shine"
       pieces for hearts and three narrow bands for pot.
       From lavender fabric, cut two rainbow pieces.
    8. From fusing material, cut one piece for each part of
       applique.
    9. From batting, cut one 41½" x 33½" piece.
B. Construct applique section:
    1. Using dressmaker's pen, mark placement for appli-
       que on blue 35½" x 17½" piece; see Diagram 1. Place
       fusing material pieces between WRONG sides of
       stem pieces and RIGHT side of blue piece. Fuse
       according to manufacturer's directions.
    2. Fuse hearts, pots and rainbow pieces.
    3. Fuse leaves, "shine" pieces and wide bands. Fuse
       narrow bands over wide bands.

(Continued)

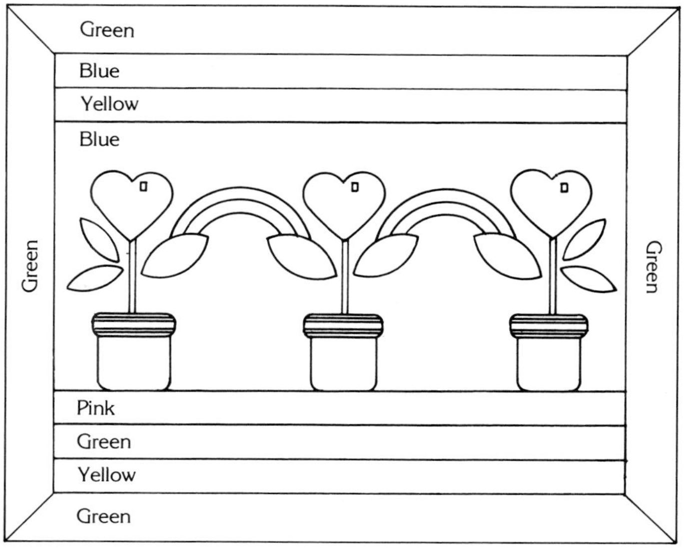

4. Machine satin stitch edges of design pieces. Stitch with pink thread around hearts and "shine" pieces. Stitch with green thread around leaves, stems and wide bands on pots. Stitch with yellow thread around pots, including lower edges of brim. Stitch edges of narrow bands with bright blue thread.

C. Construct wallhanging:

1. RIGHT sides of one blue and one yellow strip together, stitch one long edge with ¼" seam. Press seams toward blue strip. Stitch blue applique piece to second edge of yellow strip. Press seams toward blue applique piece.

2. Stitch pink strip to bottom edge of applique piece, then green 2½" wide strip, and yellow strip.

3. Mark centers of each edge of wallhanging and of green border strips. RIGHT sides together, match center of one long green strip to center of top of wallhanging. Stitch with ¼" seam to within ¼" of each corner edge; backstitch. Repeat with remaining border strips.

4. To miter corners, fold RIGHT sides of two adjacent strips together and stitch at 45-degree angle; see Diagram 2. Trim seam to ¼" seam allowance; press. Repeat for each corner.

5. Baste batting to WRONG side of wallhanging front. RIGHT sides of wallhanging front and yellow piece for back together, stitch with ¼" seam, leaving 26" opening on bottom edge. Trim batting from seam allowance. Trim corners. Turn and slip stitch opening closed.

6. Baste wallhanging thoroughly. Machine quilt on seam line inside green border and seam lines of strips, using desired thread color. Also, machine quilt around hearts, stems and flower pots.

7. From yellow ribbon, cut two 15" lengths; set aside. Slip stitch remaining yellow ribbon over seam line of pink and green strips.

8. From blue dot ribbon, cut three 15" lengths; set aside. Slip stitch remaining blue dot ribbon over seam line of green and yellow strips.

9. Cut pink ribbon into three equal lengths. Handling two pink and one green ribbon lengths as one, tie in bow and tack to right side of brim on one flower pot. Repeat with one blue dot and two yellow ribbon lengths and one pink and two blue dot ribbon lengths.

10. RIGHT sides together, stitch long edge and one end of one yellow piece for loop; turn. Slip stitch opening closed. Repeat with remaining loop pieces. Fold each strip in half. Tack to wallhanging back along upper edge, spacing evenly. Insert dowel for hanging.

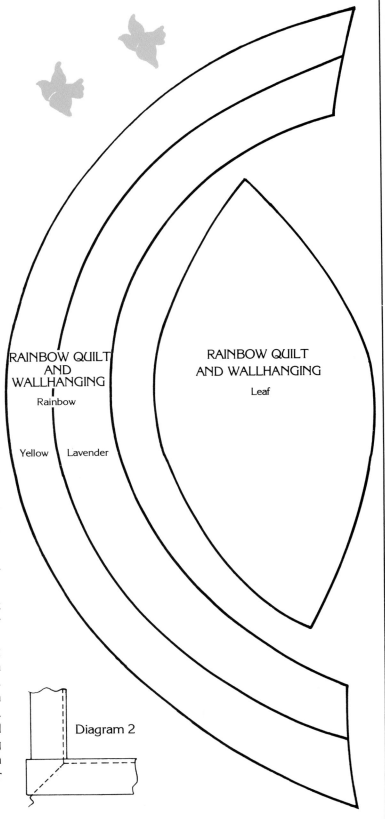

RAINBOW QUILT AND WALLHANGING

Rainbow

Yellow Lavender

RAINBOW QUILT AND WALLHANGING

Leaf

Diagram 2

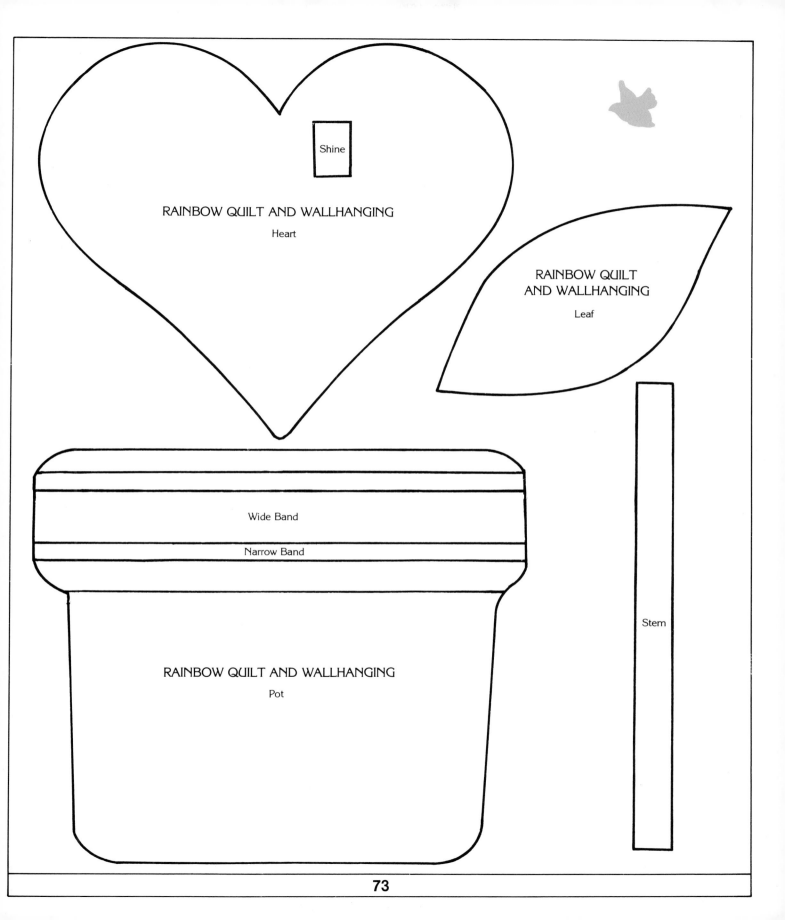

RAINBOW QUILT AND WALLHANGING

Heart

Shine

RAINBOW QUILT
AND WALLHANGING

Leaf

Wide Band

Narrow Band

RAINBOW QUILT AND WALLHANGING

Pot

Stem

The rainbow quilt

Materials needed:

3 yds. 45" yellow fabric; matching thread
⅝ yd. 45" blue fabric
½ yd. 45" green fabric; matching thread
⅜ yd. 45" purple fabric
⅜ yd. 45" pink fabric; matching thread
¼ yd. 45" apricot fabric
Small pieces yellow print, pink print, white with pink dot and pink with bright pink dot fabrics for applique
Bright blue thread
Fusing material
Batting
Dressmaker's pen
Tracing paper for patterns

A. Prepare fabric:
1. Make pattern for applique.
2. From yellow fabric, cut two 30" x 52" pieces for quilt back which wrap around to form border on quilt front.
3. From blue fabric, cut two 4" x 39" strips, two 4" x 28" strips and one 10" x 15" piece for center panel.
4. From green fabric, cut two 4" x 45" and two 4" x 34" strips.
5. From purple fabric, cut two 4" x 33" strips and two 4" x 22" strips.
6. From pink fabric, cut two 4" x 27" strips and two 4" x 16" strips.
7. From apricot fabric, cut two 4" x 21" strips and two 4" x 10" strips.
8. From remaining green fabric, cut two leaves and one stem piece. From remaining pink fabric, cut wide band on pot.
9. From pink print fabric, cut heart. From yellow print fabric, cut pot. From white with pink dot fabric, cut "shine" on heart. From pink with bright pink dot, cut narrow band on pot.
10. From fusing material, cut one piece for each part of applique.
11. From batting, cut one 45" x 50" piece.

B. Construct center panel:
1. Mark placement for applique design in center of 10" x 15" blue center panel. Place fusing material between WRONG side of stem piece and RIGHT side of center panel. Fuse according to manufacturer's directions.
2. Fuse heart, leaves and pot.
3. Fuse "shine" and wide band. Fuse narrow band over wide band.
4. Machine satin stitch edges of each design piece. Stitch with pink thread around heart and "shine". Stitch with green thread around leaves, stem and wide band on pot. Stitch with yellow thread around pot, including lower edge of brim. Stitch edges of narrow band with bright blue thread.

C. Construct quilt:
1. RIGHT sides of two yellow pieces together, stitch one 52" edge with ½" seam. Press seam open. Mark centers of all edges.
2. Mark centers of long edges of every strip. Also mark centers of each edge of center panel.
3. RIGHT sides together, match centers of shorter apricot pieces to top and bottom of center panel. Stitch with ½" seam. Open out flat with seams toward center.
4. RIGHT sides together, match centers of longer apricot pieces to sides of center panel. Stitch with ½" seam, crossing ends of shorter apricot pieces.
5. Repeat Steps C3 and C4 with remaining strips, stitching shorter pairs of strips to the top and bottoms and longer strips to sides of design. Next to apricot, stitch pink, then lavender, blue and green strips. Press all seams toward center.
6. Place yellow quilt back WRONG side up on flat surface. Center batting, then quilt front, RIGHT side up, over quilt back. Baste thoroughly.
7. Stitch around outside of quilt on green strip ½" from raw edge. Fold quilt back to quilt front, forming 3" wide border; slip stitch over seam lines, mitering corners.
8. With yellow thread, make two small stitches through all layers of quilt at 3" intervals along seam lines of strips. Remove basting.

Opposite page: A Bear To Treasure, which is easy to make, will provide pleasure for playtime hours, while The Rainbow Quilt provides comfort for sleeping hours.

Sunsuit

Designed to fit child who weighs about 20 pounds.

Materials needed:
 1½ yds. 45" yellow fabric; matching thread
 Small piece turquoise fabric
 1 yd. ⅛" wide satin ribbon
 Light turquoise and yellow embroidery floss
 1⅛ yds. ⅜" wide white lace
 ½ yd. ⅛" wide elastic
 2½ yds. small cording
 Fusing material
 Dressmaker's pen
 Tracing paper for patterns

A. Prepare fabric:
 1. Enlarge and make sunsuit body pattern. Also make bird pattern, transferring all information.
 2. From yellow fabric, cut two body pieces like pattern and four 2½" x 6½" pieces for yoke. Also cut 1" wide bias strips, piecing as needed, to equal 85".
 3. From turquoise fabric and fusing material, cut three birds.

B. Construct sunsuit:
 1. From bias strip, cut one 65" length. To make tubing for shoulder ties, fold RIGHT sides of bias around cord. With 1" of cord extending beyond end of bias, stitch with zipper foot across cord and beyond end of bias. Trim seam allowance to ⅛"; see Diagram 1. To turn, draw enclosed cord out of tubing; see Diagram 2. Trim stitched end and remove 1" of cord.

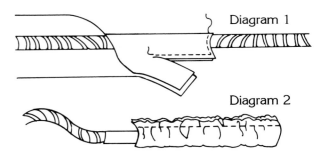

Diagram 1

Diagram 2

 2. With dressmaker's pen, center and trace pattern for placement of birds on RIGHT side of one yoke piece; see photo. With fusing material between bird and yoke, fuse one bird at a time according to manufacturer's instructions.

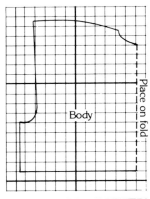

SUNSUIT BODY PATTERN
1 square = 1"

 3. With one strand turquoise embroidery floss, sew small blanket stitches around wing and body of each bird. With one strand yellow floss, sew French knot for eyes, wrapping floss around needle once.
 4. From tubing, cut eight 8" pieces. Group in pairs. Pin one pair to each upper outside corner of RIGHT side of front and back of yoke pieces, raw edges matching and ¼" from end.
 5. RIGHT side of yoke front and second yoke together, stitch side and top edges with ¼" seam. Clip corners; turn; press. Repeat for yoke back.
 6. Cut ribbon into three equal lengths. Knot each end. Fold each piece in half. Pin fold to seam allowance of yoke front below each bird.
 7. With two body pieces together, stitch curved edges with French seam. To make French seam, place WRONG sides together and stitch ¼" seam. Trim to ⅛". Place RIGHT sides together; stitch ¼" from first stitching. Also make French seam in crotch.
 8. Cut two 7½" pieces of bias. RIGHT sides of one bias strip and armhole together, stitch with ¼" seam. Fold double to WRONG side and slip stitch. Repeat for second armhole.
 9. Stitch gathering thread at top of front and back of sunsuit body to center RIGHT sides of each yoke. Stitch with ½" seam to outside yoke only, catching fold of ribbons in seam on front. Fold ½" under on inside yoke lining and slip stitch.
 10. At leg, fold fabric 1¼" to inside. Fold raw edge under ¼" and top stitch close to fold, leaving 1" opening. Complete casing by stitching second row parallel to and ¼" from first, leaving no opening; press. By hand or machine, stitch trim to fold. Measure child's leg; cut elastic this measurement plus ½". Thread elastic into casing; secure ends. Stitch opening closed. Repeat for second leg.

A bear to treasure

Materials needed:
- ⅜ yd. 45" plaid fabric; matching thread
- ⅝ yd. 1½" wide ribbon
- Stuffing
- Dressmaker's pen
- Tracing paper for patterns

Instructions:

1. Make patterns for bear head front, head back, ear, body front, body back, body gusset, arm and leg. Transfer all information.
2. From plaid fabric, cut pieces as indicated on patterns.
3. RIGHT sides of two leg pieces together, stitch with ¼" seam, leaving top edge open; turn. Repeat for second leg. RIGHT sides of two arm pieces together, stitch with ¼" seam, leaving top edge open; turn. Repeat for second arm.
4. Stuff arms and legs firmly, stopping ¾" from openings. Match and pin seams of legs at opening; machine baste opening closed. Pin arms with seams on either side; baste opening closed.
5. RIGHT sides of head back pieces together, stitch center back with ¼" seam. RIGHT sides of head front pieces together, stitch center front with ¼" seam.
6. RIGHT sides of two ear pieces together, stitch with ⅛" seam, leaving bottom edge open. Clip curved seam allowances; turn. Pin tucks in ears. RIGHT sides together and matching raw edges, pin ears to head front, 1½" each side of top center seam.
7. RIGHT sides fo head front and back pieces together, stitch with ¼" seam, leaving neck edge of head open. Clip curved seam allowances; turn.
8. RIGHT sides of body pieces together, stitch center back with ¼" seam. RIGHT sides of body front pieces together, stitch center front with ¼" seam.
9. RIGHT sides together, pin arms to body front ½" from top corner. RIGHT sides of body front and back together, stitch with ¼" seam, leaving neck and gusset areas open.
10. RIGHT sides of head and body neck edges together, match seams; pin. Stitch ¼" seam around neck twice. Turn.
11. Pin legs, with toes pointing forward, on bottom edge of body front ½" from center seam. RIGHT sides of body front and gusset together, stitch with ¼" seam. Turn.
12. Stuff bear head, then body, firmly. Fold under ¼" on body back and gusset and slip stitch securely.
13. Tie ribbon in bow around bear's neck.

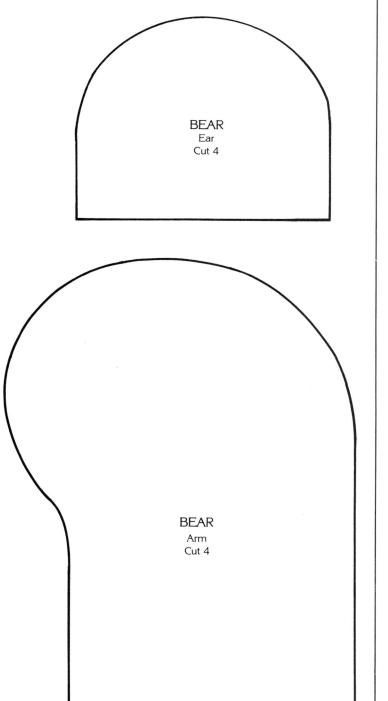

BEAR
Ear
Cut 4

BEAR
Arm
Cut 4

Opening

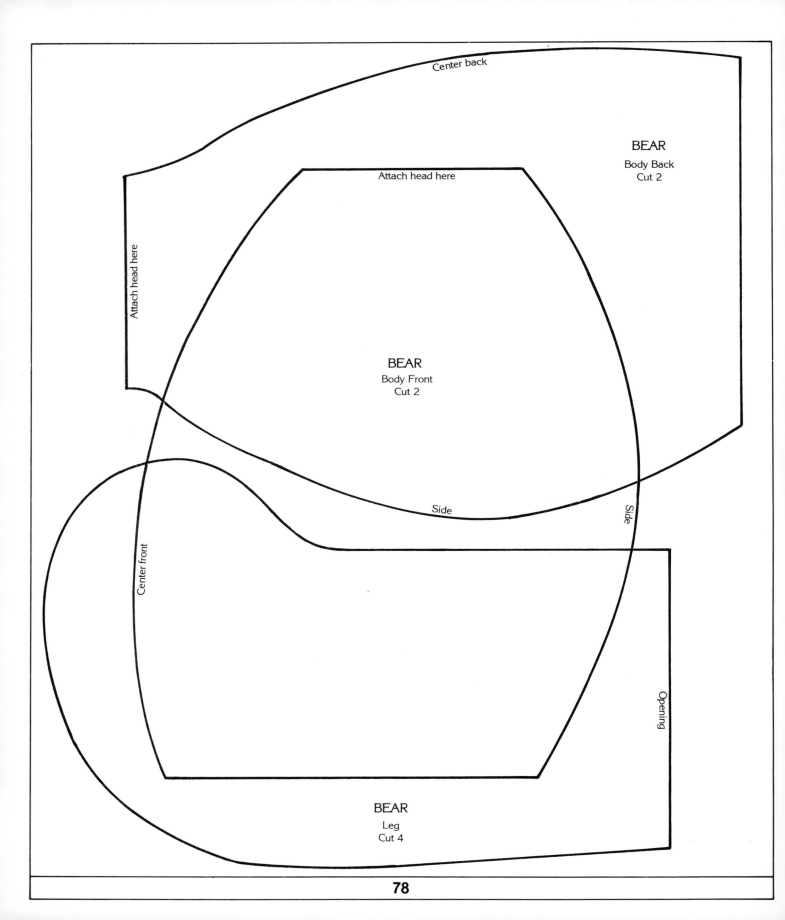

Center back

BEAR
Body Back
Cut 2

Attach head here

Attach head here

BEAR
Body Front
Cut 2

Side

Side

Center front

Opening

BEAR

Leg
Cut 4

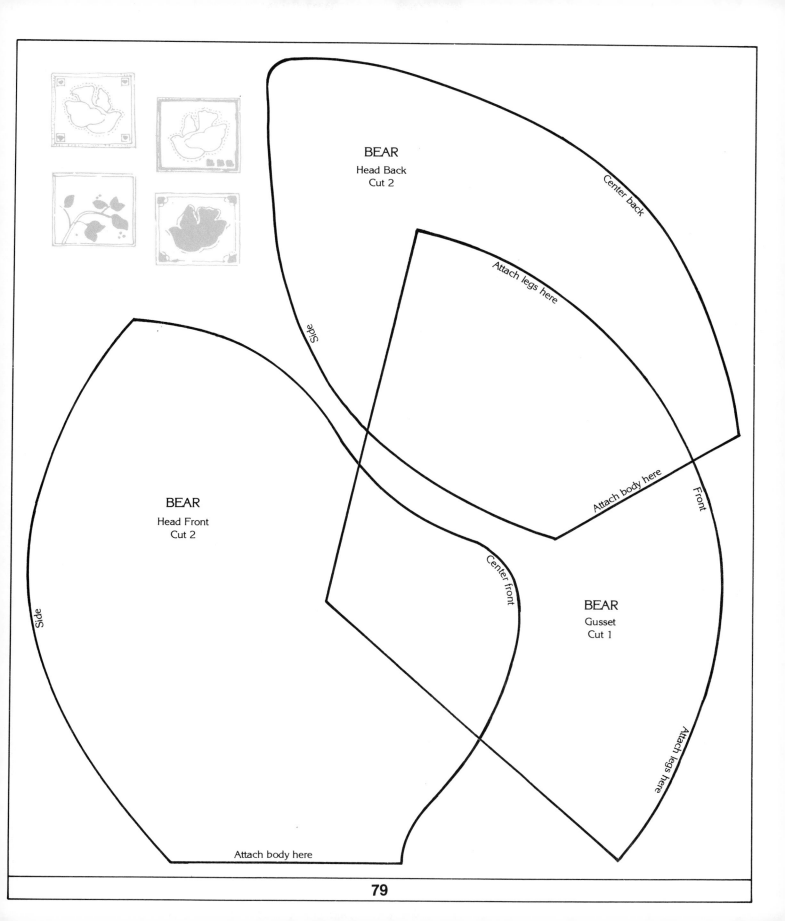

BEAR
Head Back
Cut 2

Center back

Attach legs here

Side

BEAR
Head Front
Cut 2

Attach body here

Front

Center front

BEAR
Gusset
Cut 1

Side

Attach legs here

Attach body here

June

Special secrets and magical things,
Bright summer sun and butterfly wings,
Surprises that wait like a gold cocoon
Are there for you, my child of June.

Butterflies are not just for June! These Woven Ribbon Butterflies, can also be used for a mobile, a sun-catcher or for the finishing touch on a gift.

Opposite page: Butterflies and flowers, straight from the mountains, have landed on A Quilt Of Butterflies and the Tulip Pillow. A Summer Tote is filled with an afternoon's picnic supplies. The Woven Ribbon Butterfly is a keepsake reminiscent of the day.

A quilt of butterflies

Materials needed:
  4½ yds. 45" white polished cotton fabric; matching thread
  ⅛ yd. 45" purple print fabric; matching thread
  ⅛ yd. 45" blue fabric; matching thread
  ⅛ yd. 45" red seersucker fabric; matching thread
  ⅛ yd. 45" red/white check print seersucker fabric
  Batting
  Fusing material
  White quilting thread
  Safety pins
  Dressmaker's pen
  Tracing paper for patterns

A. Prepare fabric:
  1. Make patterns for entire butterfly, tulip, heart and small circle.
  2. From white fabric, cut two 40" x 40" pieces. Also cut 3" wide bias strips, piecing as needed, to equal 10 yds.
  3. From purple fabric, cut twelve tulips and four butterfly bodies.
  4. From blue fabric, cut twelve hearts.
  5. From red seersucker, cut eight lower wings and twenty-four circles.
  6. From red/white seersucker, cut eight upper wings.
  7. From batting, cut one 40" x 40" piece.
  8. From fusing material, cut one for each piece cut in Steps A3 through A6.
B. Construct quilt:
  1. On one white piece, mark center and quarters with dressmaker's pen. Following measurements in Diagram 1, place flowers and hearts on quilt. With fusing material between fabric pieces and quilt top, fuse according to manufacturer's instructions. Fuse circles; see Diagram 1.

2. Fuse butterfly wings, then body, in each corner; see Diagram 1.
3. With matching thread and wide satin stitch, machine applique all fused pieces. With dressmaker's pen, mark flower stems and butterfly antennae. Machine stitch with purple thread and wide satin stitch; see photo.
4. With dressmaker's pen, mark scallops above each flower; see pattern. Also mark quilting lines; see Diagram 1.
5. Place second white piece, WRONG side up, on flat surface, cover with batting, and place quilt top, RIGHT side up, over batting. Baste thoroughly.
6. With quilting thread, quilt by hand on each pen line and around each appliqued piece, including butterfly bodies and antennae; see photo.
7. RIGHT sides together, stitch ends of bias strip with ½" seam to make one continuous piece. Stitch gathering threads on each edge of entire piece and fold bias strip into quarters; mark with safety pins.
8. RIGHT sides of bias and quilt top together, match quarter marks to corners; pin. Pulling all four bobbin threads at once, gather one quarter of bias at a time to equal 40". Stitch one edge of bias to quilt through all layers with ½" seam. Repeat for each quarter, allowing slightly more fullness at corners.
9. Fold bias to back of quilt and fold raw edge under ½". Slip stitch to quilt back. Remove gathering threads which show.

Diagram 1

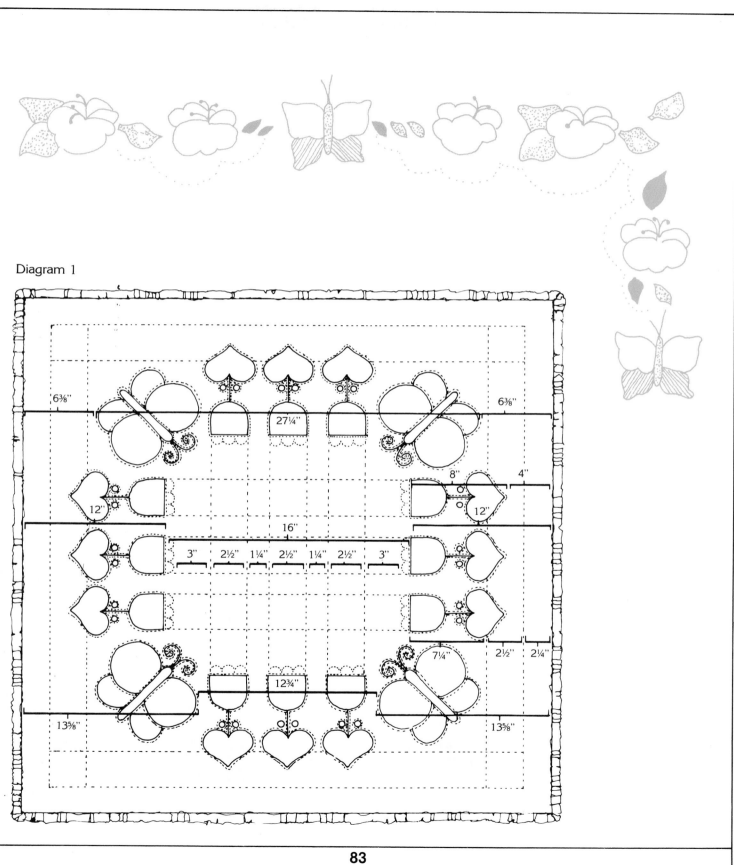

6⅜" 27¼" 6⅜"
8" 4"
12" 12"
16"
3" 2½" 1¼" 2½" 1¼" 2½" 3"
2½" 2¼"
7¼"
12¾"
13⅝" 13⅝"

Tulip pillow

Materials needed:
  1⅜ yds. 45" blue fabric; matching thread
  Small pieces purple and red print fabric
  Small piece white fabric; matching thread
  One 12½" x 15½" piece muslin
  One 12½" x 15½" piece fleece
  Stuffing
  Fusing material
  Tracing paper for patterns

A. Prepare fabric:
  1. Make patterns for tulip, heart and small circle.
  2. From blue fabric, cut two 12½" x 15½" pieces. Also cut 7" wide bias strips, piecing as needed, to equal 3¾ yds.
  3. From purple fabric, cut three tulips; from red fabric, cut three hearts; from white fabric, cut six circles.
  4. From fusing material, cut one for each piece cut in Step A3.

B. Construct pillow:
  1. Place one 12½" x 15½" piece blue fabric, RIGHT side up, on flat surface. Center and place tulips, hearts and circles on blue fabric with fusing material under each piece; see photo. Fuse according to manufacturer's instructions.
  2. With white thread and wide satin stitch, machine applique all fused pieces. Machine satin stitch flower stem.
  3. Place muslin on flat surface. Center fleece, then appliqued pillow top, RIGHT side up, over muslin; baste. With one strand of white thread, quilt ⅛" outside all satin stitching. Mark and quilt scallops above each flower; see pattern.
  4. RIGHT sides together, stitch 7" ends of bias strip with ½" seam to form one continuous piece. Fold in half with WRONG sides together to measure 3½"; press. Mark bias in quarters. Sew gathering threads along raw edge of strip. Gather to 56".
  5. Mark center of each side of pillow top. Pin bias strip to RIGHT side of pillow front, matching raw edges and marks. Disperse fullness evenly. Stitch with ½" seam.
  6. RIGHT sides of pillow front and remaining blue fabric piece together, stitch on stitching line of bias strip, leaving 5" opening. Clip corners, turn and stuff firmly. Slip stitch opening closed.

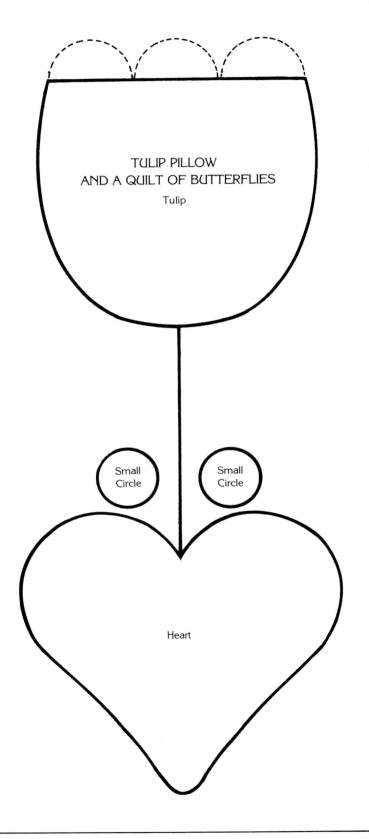

TULIP PILLOW
AND A QUILT OF BUTTERFLIES
Tulip

Small Circle

Small Circle

Heart

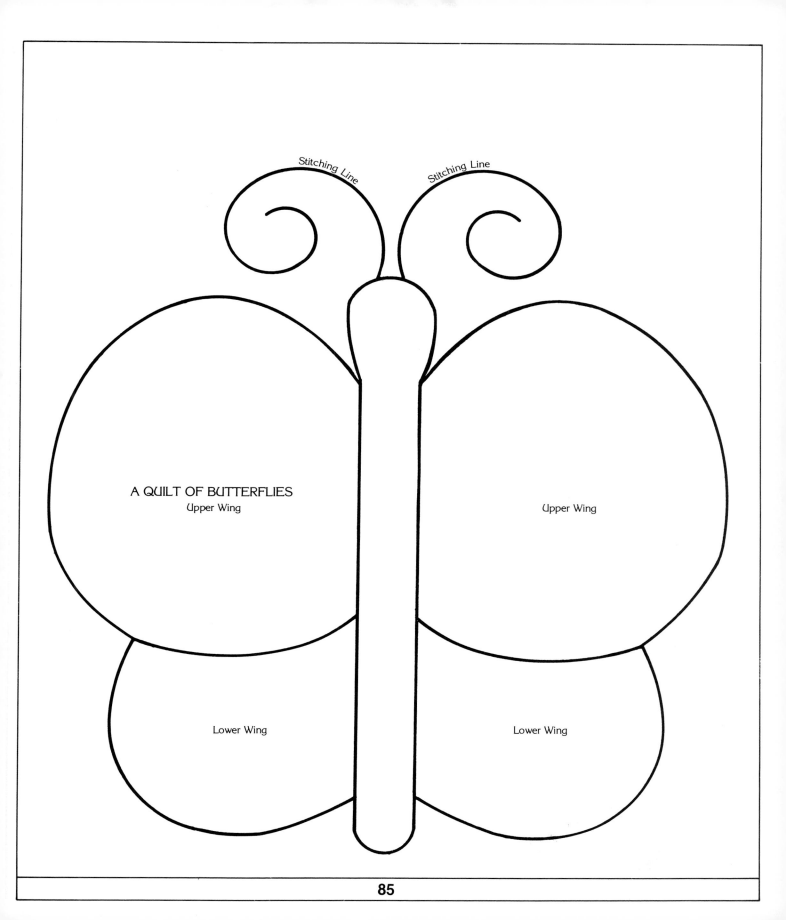

A QUILT OF BUTTERFLIES
Upper Wing

Stitching Line

Stitching Line

Upper Wing

Lower Wing

Lower Wing

A summer tote

Materials needed for tote:
1⅜ yd. 45" blue fabric; matching thread
⅞ yd. 45" white eyelet fabric with border design
1 yd. ⅜" wide flat white trim
1½ yds. ½" wide red satin ribbon
½ yd. polyester fleece
¼ yd. fusible interfacing for handles

Materials needed for heart:
4½ yds. ⅛" wide white satin ribbon; matching thread
⅝ yd. 1/16" wide purple satin ribbon
½ yd. 1/16" wide red satin ribbon
⅜ yd. ⅛" wide blue satin ribbon
One 4" x 4" piece fusing material
One 4" x 4" piece blue fabric
Tracing paper for pattern

A. Prepare fabric:
1. From blue fabric, cut three 15" x 31" pieces for tote outside, lining and pocket panel. Also cut two 2" x 22" pieces for handles.
2. From eyelet, cut one 12" x 31" piece.
3. From fleece, cut one 15" x 31" piece.
4. From interfacing, cut two 2" x 22" pieces.

B. Construct tote:
1. For pocket piece, fold one 15" x 31" piece lengthwise with WRONG sides together; press.
2. Fuse interfacing to WRONG sides of 2" x 22" pieces. RIGHT sides together, stitch 22" edges with ¼" seam. Turn and press. Repeat for second piece.
3. Pin eyelet to RIGHT side of one 15" x 31" piece with raw edge of eyelet aligned with bottom edge of blue fabric. Pin fleece to WRONG side of blue fabric. Fold all layers with eyelet sides together and stitch bottom and side with ¼" seam.
4. To make square corner, fold bag so side seam and bottom seam meet. Stitch according to Diagram 1. Repeat for second corner.
5. Match raw edge of pocket piece to one long edge of 15" x 32" lining piece; pin. To make pockets, stitch between raw edge and fold at desired intervals.
6. RIGHT sides of pocket/lining piece together, stitch side and bottom with ¼" seam, leaving 4" opening. Make square corners; see Step B4.
7. Pin raw ends of handle pieces to top edge of tote. Slide lining over tote outside, matching side seams; pin. Stitch with ¼" seam around top edge. Turn through opening in lining. Slip stitch opening closed.

8. Fold red ribbon into 4" wide loops. Tack to handle of tote.

C. Construct heart:
1. Make pattern for heart, page 84.
2. Place fabric piece, WRONG side up, on ironing board. Place fusing material over fabric and pin both layers to ironing board.
3. Working with 4" lengths of white, purple and red ribbon, lay ribbon lengths horizontally over fusing material with edges of ribbons not quite touching, integrating purple and red ribbons as desired. Pin left ends of ribbons to ironing board; see Diagram 2.

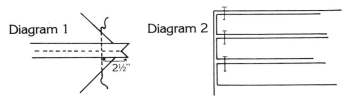

Diagram 1   Diagram 2

4. Working with 4" lengths of white, purple and red ribbon, lay ribbon lengths vertically over ribbons and fusing material with edges of ribbons not quite touching, integrating purple and red ribbons as desired. Pin top ends of ribbons to ironing board; see Diagram 3.

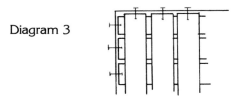

Diagram 3

5. Weave ribbons; see Diagram 4. Pin ribbon ends in place. Place pressing cloth over ribbons. Fuse ribbons to fabric according to manufacturer's instructions.

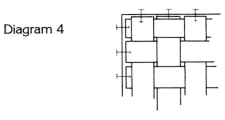

Diagram 4

6. Trace heart pattern diagonally over woven ribbons with dressmaker's pen. Using close satin stitch, stitch over pen line. Trim woven ribbons close to stitching and satin stitch edges again.
7. Tack one end of blue ribbon to back of heart. Fold red ribbon into four 4" wide loops. Tie second end of blue ribbon around center of loops to form bow. Tie blue ribbon around handle of tote bag. Tack bow to handle.

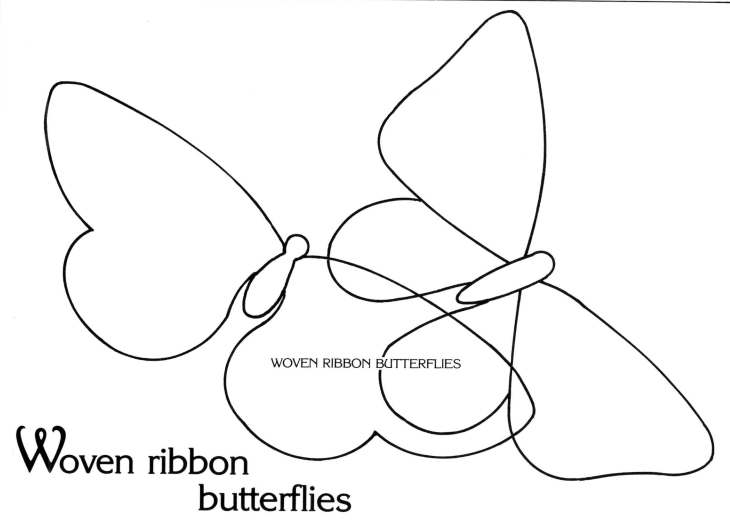

WOVEN RIBBON BUTTERFLIES

Woven ribbon butterflies

Materials needed for one:
  6¾ yds. ⅛" wide satin ribbon (the butterflies shown in the
    photo use a combination of ribbon colors)
  Two 5" x 6" pieces fabric to match ribbons; matching
    thread
  One 4" length thin wire
  One 5" x 6" piece fusing material
  One 18" length ⅛" wide wooden dowel
  White glue
  Tracing paper for pattern

1. Make pattern for butterfly.
2. Place one fabric piece, RIGHT side up, on ironing board
   with 5" edge place horizontally. Place fusing material over
   fabric and pin both layers to ironing board.
3. Working with 5" lengths of ribbon, lay ribbon lengths horizontally over fusing material with edges of ribbons not
   quite touching. Pin left ends of ribbons to ironing board;
   see Diagram 2; page 86.

4. Working with 6" lengths of ribbon, lay ribbons lengths
   vertically over ribbons and fusing material with edges of
   ribbons not quite touching. Pin top ends of ribbons to
   ironing board; see Diagram 3.
5. Weave ribbons; see Diagram 4. Pin ribbon ends in place.
   Place pressing cloth over ribbons. Fuse ribbons to fabric
   according to manufacturer's instructions.
6. Place butterfly pattern diagonally over woven ribbons.
   From woven ribbons, cut one butterfly.
7. Place remaining fabric piece, WRONG side up, on flat surface. Place ribbon butterfly, RIGHT side up, over fabric.
   Insert wire beneath ribbon butterfly piece, placing wire
   across top of butterfly.
8. Using close satin stitch, stitch edges of butterfly. Trim
   fabric back piece close to stitching and satin stitch edges
   again. Also satin stitch lines shown on pattern.
9. Glue one end of dowel to back of butterfly. Shape wings by
   folding wire.

July

July's child and her nighttime friends
Are always there at a summer day's end.
They play 'til morn, joyous and sweet,
And live together on Good Children Street.

A Mobile Of Ducks is a reminder of a warm July day spent feeding the ducks at Grandpa's pond. Back home on Good Children Street, the summer's days are recorded in cross-stitch and satin ribbons.

Opposite page: An Aqua Quilt makes an inviting setting for little girls to braid one another's hair. More Ducks, a crib toy or garland, and A Mobile Of Ducks repeat the motif in the quilt. Fabric from the quilt is used to cover the mat on Good Children Street. The apricot bunny, the pink pig and lavender bear are all Animal Tie-Ons which the girls can trade between pillows.

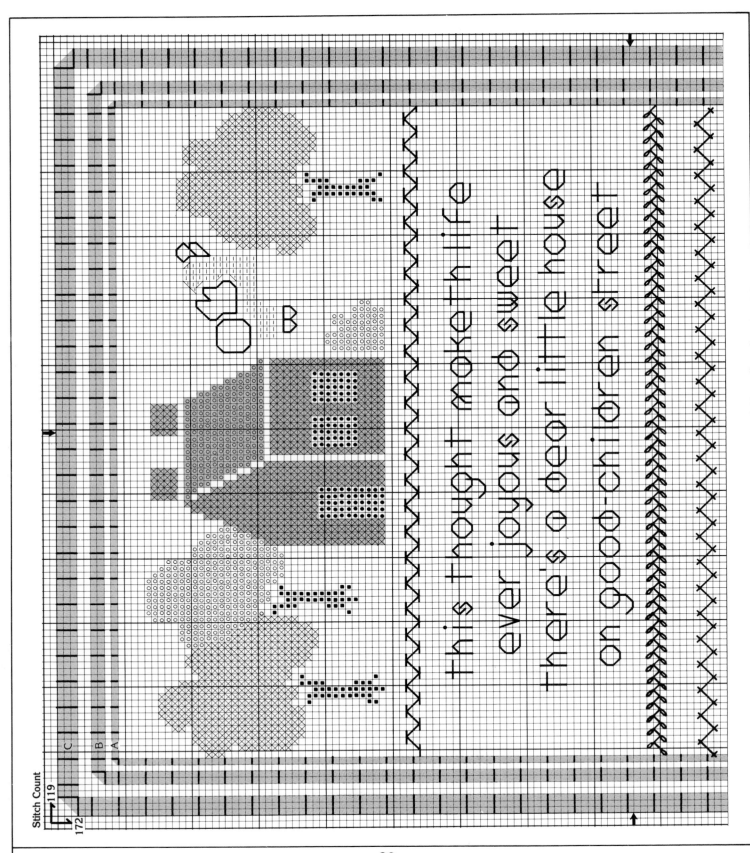

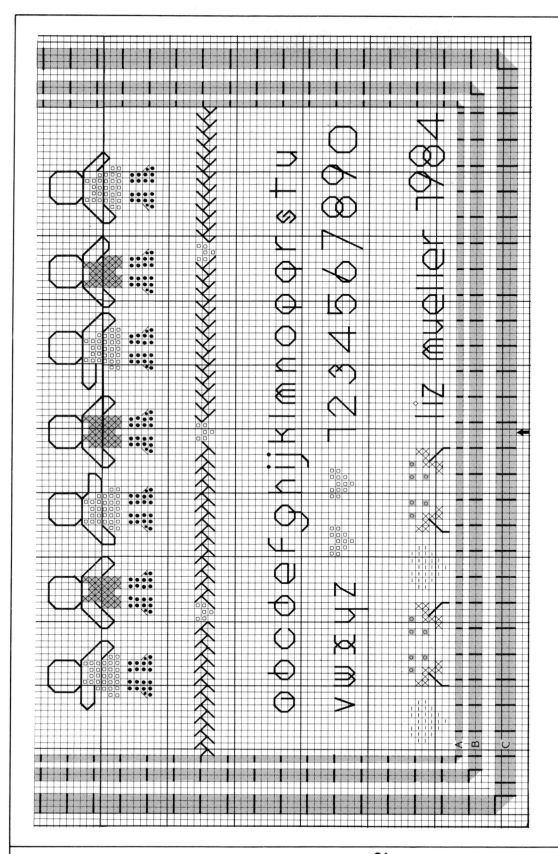

abcdefghijklmnopqrstu
vwxyz
1234567890

liz mueller 1984

A
B
C

Good children street

Good children street

Cover sample: Stitched on White Linda 27 over two threads. Finished design size is 8¾" x 12¾". Cut fabric 15" x 19". Finished design size using other fabrics are — Aida 11: 10⅞" x 15⅝"; Aida 14: 8½" x 12¼"; Aida 18: 6⅝" x 9½"; Hardanger 22: 5⅜" x 7⅞".

Also needed:
1¼ yds. 1/16" wide light orchid satin ribbon; matching floss
1¼ yds. ⅛" wide iris satin ribbon
1⅜ yds. ¼" wide grape satin ribbon

BATES		DMC	(used for cover sample)
		Step One: Cross-stitch (two strands)	
85	▫	3609	Plum · ultra lt.
87	◦	3607	Plum · lt.
118	☒	340	Blue Violet · med.
185	– ╱	964	Seagreen · lt.
203	◦	954	Nile Green
205	☒	911	Emerald Green · med.
914	●	3064	Sportsman Flesh · med.
401	● ╱	844	Beaver Gray · ultra dk.
		Step Two: Back Stitch (one strand)	
110		208	Lavender · vy. dk. (name and date)
229		909	Emerald Green · vy. dk. (alphabet and poem)
401		844	Beaver Gray · ultra dk. (all else)
		Step Three: French Knots (one strand)	
110	◦	208	Lavender · vy. dk. (name)
229	●	909	Emerald Green · vy. dk. (alphabet and poem)
		Step Four: Embroidery Stitches	
85		3609	Plum · ultra lt. (Chevron stitch)
118		340	Blue Violet · med. (Chained feather stitch)
85		3609	Plum · ultra lt. (Herringbone stitch)
185		964	Seagreen · lt. (Back stitch)

Step Five: Ribbon Work
Beginning at lower right corner, thread one end of ribbon to WRONG side and tack. Lay ribbon in place on bottom edge of stitched piece and couch with one strand of matching floss as indicated on graph. Continue around stitched piece, folding ribbon at corners. Ending at lower right corner, thread second ribbon end to WRONG side and tack.

A		Light Orchid Ribbon
B		Iris Ribbon
C		Grape Ribbon

More ducks...

GARLAND

Materials needed for a garland of five ducks:
½ yd. 45" aqua print fabric; matching thread
¼ yd. 45" aqua check fabric
⅛ yd. 45" yellow check fabric; matching thread
4½ yds. ¼" wide yellow satin ribbon
Fusing material
Batting
Dressmaker's pen
Tracing paper for patterns

A. Prepare fabric:
1. Make patterns for duck, wing and bill, page 97.
2. Using dressmaker's pen, trace duck pattern onto RIGHT side of aqua print fabric to make five ducks facing right and five ducks facing left. Roughly cut duck shapes outside of pen lines.
3. From aqua check fabric, cut ten wing pieces.
4. From yellow check fabric, cut ten bill pieces.
5. From fusing material, cut ten wing pieces and ten bill pieces.
6. From batting, cut five duck pieces.

B. Construct ducks:
1. Place one wing piece, RIGHT side up, over RIGHT side of one aqua print duck with fusing material between layers. Fuse according to manufacturer's instructions. Using aqua thread and widest setting, machine satin stitch twice around wing. Repeat with remaining duck and wing pieces.
2. Fuse one bill to one duck. Using yellow thread, machine satin stitch twice around bill. Repeat.
3. Match WRONG sides of two corresponding ducks. Insert batting between layers; pin, making sure outside pen lines of ducks match. Using yellow thread for bill and aqua thread for remainder of duck, machine satin stitch around duck. Cut outside edge of design near satin stitching and stitch edge again. Repeat.
4. Cut one 20" length of ribbon. To connect two ducks, tack ribbon; see Diagram 1. Repeat to connect five ducks.

Diagram 1

5. For end ties, cut remaining ribbon into two equal lengths. Tie a bow 6" from one end; tack to end ducks.

An aqua quilt

Materials needed:
  2⅞ yds. 45" aqua fabric; matching thread
  ⅝ yd. 45" white fabric; matching thread
  Batting
  Dressmaker's pen
  Tracing paper for pattern

A. Prepare fabric:
  1. Make pattern for duck (page 97), transferring bill and wing lines.
  2. From aqua fabric, cut two 45" x 49½" pieces for quilt front and back.
  3. From white fabric, cut 2¼" wide bias strips, piecing as needed, to equal 5½ yds. for binding.

  4. From batting, cut one 45" x 49½" piece.
B. Construct quilt:
  1. On RIGHT side of one aqua piece for quilt front, mark quilting lines with dressmaker's pen; see Diagram 1.
  2. Place second aqua piece for quilt back, WRONG side up, on flat surface. Layer batting, then quilt front, RIGHT side up, over quilt back. Baste thoroughly.
  3. With aqua thread, machine quilt pen lines. Remove basting.
  4. RIGHT sides of binding and quilt front together, stitch with ½" seam. Fold binding double to back and slip stitch.

Diagram 1

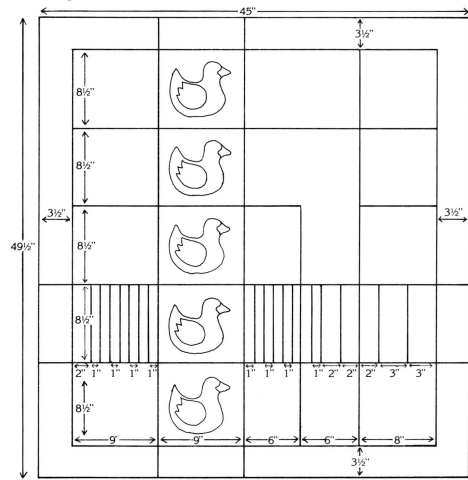

$\mathcal{A}$ mobile of ducks

Materials needed:
  ¼ yd. 45" wide aqua print fabric; matching thread
  ⅛ yd. 45" wide aqua check fabric
  Small piece yellow check fabric for beaks; matching thread
  4¾ yds. ⅛" wide yellow satin ribbon
  Small piece fusing material
  Batting
  Stuffing
  Dressmaker's pen
  Tracing paper for patterns

A. Prepare fabric:
  1. Make pattern for duck (page 97), adding ¼" seam allowance. Also make pattern for gusset.
  2. From aqua print fabric, cut six duck pieces and three gusset pieces.
  3. From aqua check fabric, cut twelve 3½" x 4½" pieces. Using dressmaker's pen, trace wing pattern onto six pieces.
  4. From yellow check fabric, cut six beak pieces.
  5. From fusing material, cut six beak pieces.
  6. From batting, cut six 3½" x 4½" pieces.
B. Construct ducks:
  1. Place one beak piece on each duck piece with fusing material between layers. Fuse according to manufacturer's instructions. Using yellow thread, satin stitch edge of beak next to duck's head.
  2. Place one batting piece between WRONG sides of one marked aqua check piece and one unmarked aqua check piece. Satin stitch around wing with matching thread. Trim fabric and batting close to stitching and satin stitch edge again. Repeat with remaining wing pieces.

  3. RIGHT sides of two duck pieces together, stitch with ¼" seam around top of duck between stars as indicated on pattern; backstitch. RIGHT sides together, stitch with ¼" seam one side of gusset piece to duck front as indicated on pattern. Repeat on second side, leaving 2½" opening. Turn. Stuff duck firmly. Slip stitch opening closed. Repeat with remaining duck pieces.
  4. Tack front edge of wing to side of duck; see pattern for placement. Repeat.
  5. Cut three 20" lengths of yellow ribbon for bows; set aside. Also cut one 48" length, one 36" length and one 26" length. Fold 48" length ribbon in half; tack fold to center top of duck; see photo. Repeat to attach 36" and 26" ribbon lengths to remaining ducks.
  6. Tie each 20" length ribbon into double bow. Tack each bow to center top of duck; see photo. Match ends of ribbons and tie in knot.

Place on fold

A MOBILE OF DUCKS
Gusset

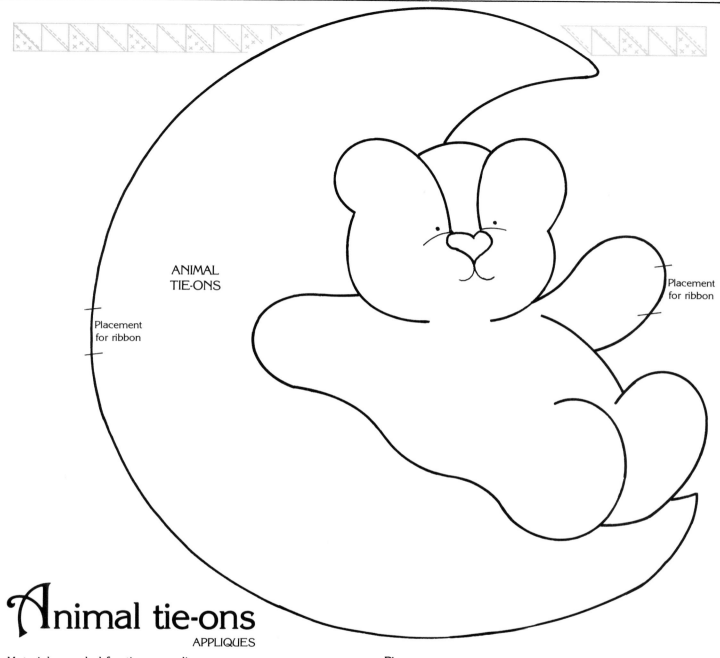

ANIMAL
TIE-ONS

Placement
for ribbon

Placement
for ribbon

Animal tie-ons
APPLIQUES

Materials needed for tie-on applique:

Rabbit:
  Two 8" x 8" pieces apricot fabric; matching thread
  Small piece white fabric for tail
  Lavender embroidery thread

Duck:
  Two 8" x 8" pieces aqua print fabric; matching thread
  Small piece aqua check fabric for wing
  Small piece yellow check fabric for beak
  Lavender embroidery floss

Pig:
  Two 8" x 8" pieces pink fabric; matching thread
  Small pieces pink fabric for ears
  Small piece white fabric for nose
  Green embroidery floss

Bear:
  Two 8" x 8" pieces lavender print fabric;
    matching thread
  Small piece lavender print fabric for bear body
  Aqua embroidery floss

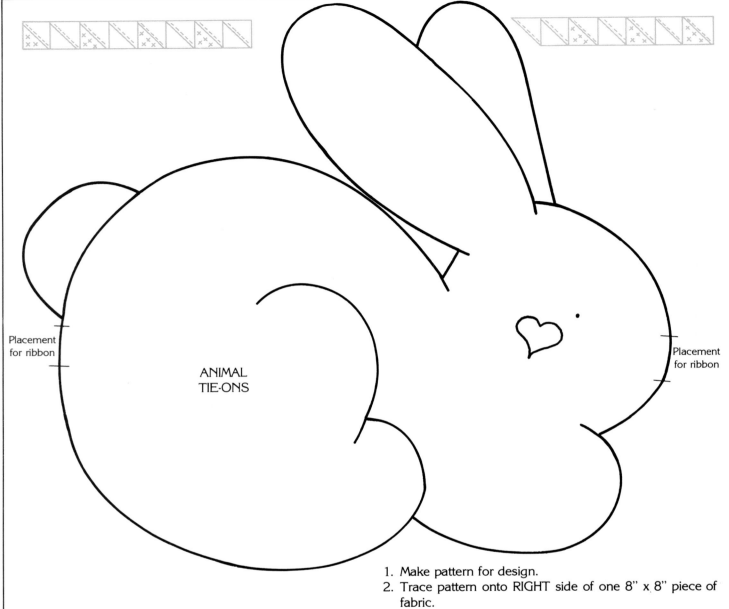

ANIMAL
TIE-ONS

Placement
for ribbon

Placement
for ribbon

Horse:
Two 8" x 8" pieces yellow fabric; matching thread
Small pieces lavender fabric for mane and tail;
 matching thread
Pink embroidery floss

For each design:
One 8" x 8" piece polyester fleece
1 yd. ½" wide white satin ribbon
Small pieces of fusing material
Dressmaker's pen
Tracing paper for patterns

1. Make pattern for design.
2. Trace pattern onto RIGHT side of one 8" x 8" piece of fabric.
3. From fabric for ears, nose, wing, beak, mane, tail or bear, cut one piece like pattern. Also cut piece from fusing material. Place piece on RIGHT side of design with fusing material between layers. Fuse according to manufacturer's instructions. Repeat for additional pieces.
4. Layer fleece between WRONG sides of 8" x 8" fabric pieces; pin securely. Satin stitch with widest setting around design, changing colors unless a contrast is desired.
5. Cut outside edge of design near satin stitching.
6. Cut ribbon length into two equal lengths. Pin one of each piece against back side of design; see pattern for placement.
7. Satin stitch each line again. Tie design onto pillow.

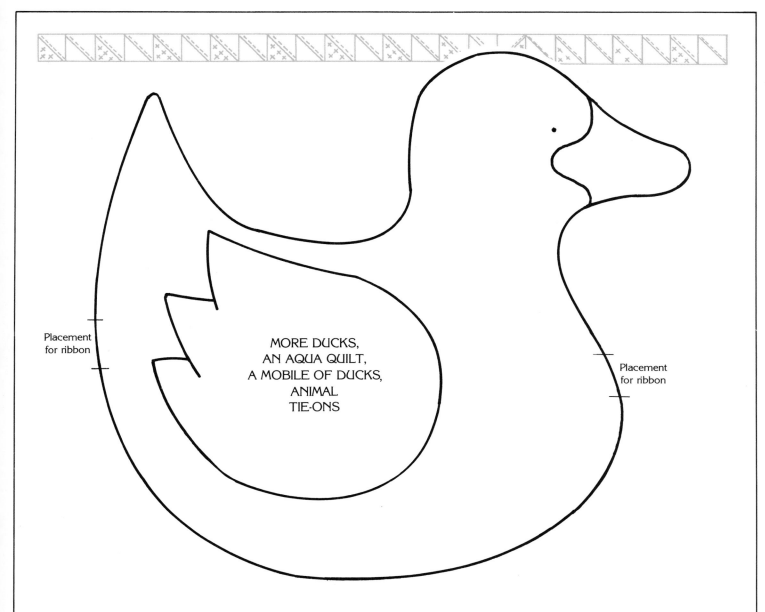

Placement for ribbon

MORE DUCKS,
AN AQUA QUILT,
A MOBILE OF DUCKS,
ANIMAL
TIE-ONS

Placement for ribbon

Animal tie-ons
PILLOWS

Materials needed for pillow:
 ⅜ yd. 45" white chintz fabric; matching thread
 1¼ yds. small cording
 1 yd. ½" wide white satin ribbon
 10" x 10" box pillow form or stuffing

1. From white fabric, cut two 11" x 11" pieces for pillow. Also cut 1¼" wide bias strips, piecing as needed, to equal 1¼ yds. for cording. Make cording; see General Instructions.

2. Stitch cording to RIGHT side of one 11" x 11" white fabric piece.

3. RIGHT sides of both 11" x 11" white pieces together, stitch on stitching line of cording, leaving 5" opening on one side. Turn. Stuff; slip stitch opening closed.

4. Tuck each corner to inside ¾". Tack cording together to form square corners.

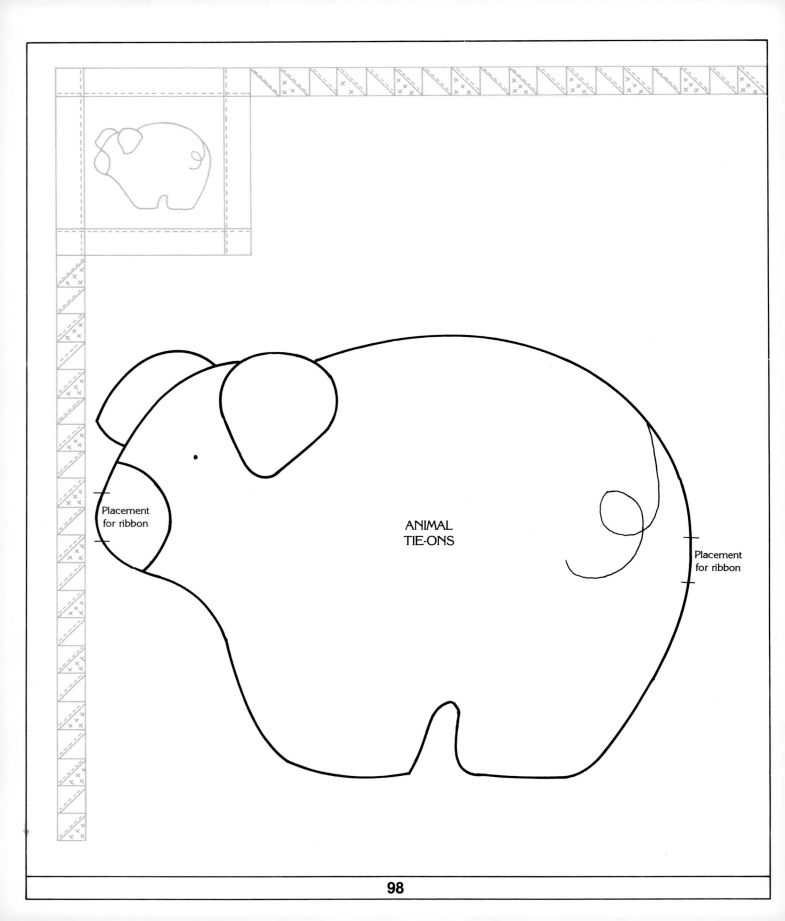

Placement for ribbon

ANIMAL
TIE-ONS

Placement for ribbon

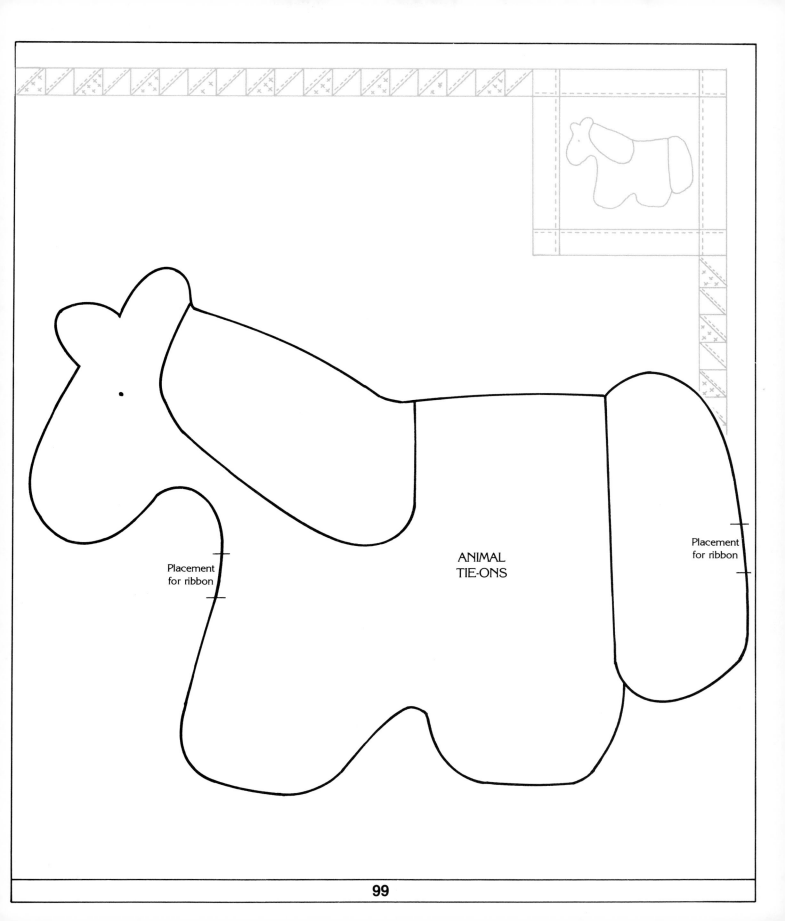

ANIMAL
TIE-ONS

Placement
for ribbon

Placement
for ribbon

August

Tender and loving is this little one,
Adorned in ribbons and the warm August sun.
Entering a world of dear doll friends,
They can share secrets 'til the long days end.

Megan, one of the Six Little Playmates, is trimmed in eyelet and has taken off her straw hat to await the arrival of a special friend.

Opposite page: Dolls and dollhouses - fabric, paper and wood - combine to make summer days hardly long enough! The fabric dolls, styled after traditional rag dolls, are Six Little Playmates and the cut-out clothing fits My Paper Doll. Good Friends expresses a sentiment appropriate for only the dearest of playmates.

only the very best of what you have to give is good enough for a friend

DOLLY DINGLE'S COUSIN MARION

Six little playmates

BODY

Note: All seams are ¼".

Materials needed:
   ¼ yd. 45" fabric for body; matching thread
   Stuffing
   Yarn; see instructions for hair
   Dark brown embroidery floss for eyes
   Pink or red crayon for cheeks
   Dressmaker's pen
   Tracing paper for patterns

A. Prepare fabric:
   1. Make patterns for head/body, arm, leg and foot, transferring all information.
   2. From fabric, cut body pieces as indicated on patterns.

B. Construct doll:
   1. RIGHT sides together, stitch two arm pieces, leaving opening as indicated on pattern. Clip seam allowance at thumb. Turn. Repeat for second arm.
   2. RIGHT sides together, match A on leg to A on foot; stitch. Fold leg/foot piece with RIGHT sides together, stitch; see Diagram 1. Turn. Fold leg with seam at center back. Repeat for second leg.
   3. Stuff lower half of leg firmly; stitch knee. Stuff remainder of leg firmly to within ½" of top. Stitch top edge. Repeat for second leg.
   4. Pin arms to RIGHT side of one body piece with hands toward center of body; see pattern. RIGHT sides of two body pieces together, with arms sandwiched between, stitch head and sides, leaving bottom edge open. Turn.
   5. Pin legs to RIGHT side of body front; see pattern. Stitch.
   6. Stuff body firmly. Turn seam allowance at bottom edge inside; slip stitch.
   7. Stuff lower half of one arm firmly; stitch elbow. Stuff upper arm moderately; slip stitch opening closed. Repeat for second arm.

8. Using matching thread, make two small tucks in front of neck to add fullness to face; see Diagram 2. Repeat for back of neck.

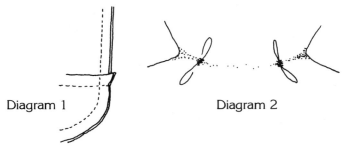

Diagram 1   Diagram 2

9. Attach yarn hair to head.
10. Using two strands of floss, make French knots for eyes, wrapping floss around needle once. Color cheeks with crayon.

PIGTAILS AND BRAIDS

Materials needed:
   One skein "fluffy" acrylic yarn; matching thread
   Large-eyed needle
   Ribbon to match clothing

1. Transfer hairline from pattern to doll head. Also draw a line down center of back of head, ending ½" above neck.
2. For hair on back of head, use 14" lengths of yarn. Thread one length onto large-eyed needle and stitch in place; see Diagram 1. Repeat with stitches close together until hairline is covered.
3. For bangs and hair on side of head, use 16" lengths of yarn. Fold each length in half. At center of forehead, place yarn on head with folded end toward face. With matching thread, tack yarn into place, leaving 1" of loop for bangs; see Diagram 2. Complete one half of head, then second half.
4. Part hair in center and pull to sides. Arrange hair in desired style before trimming ends.

For **Elizabeth**, arrange hair into pigtail on each side of head. Cut six 8" lengths of ¼" wide satin ribbon. Tie three lengths into 2" wide bows around one pigtail; see photo. Repeat for second side. Trim hair to desired length.

For **Annie**, braid hair on each side of head. Tie ends of braids with short lengths of 1/16" wide satin ribbon. Cut two 6" lengths of ¼" wide satin ribbon. Tie each length into 2" wide bows around top of braids.

For **Amanda**, braid hair on each side of head. Tie ends of braids with short lengths of yarn. Using matching thread, tack ends of braids to top center of head; see photo. Cut two 6" lengths of ⅜" wide blue grosgrain ribbon. Tie each into 2" wide bows. Tack each bow to base of braid.

For **Catherine**, tie hair into pigtail on each side of head with short length of yarn. Cut four 6" lengths of ⅛" wide satin ribbon. Tie one length into 2" wide bow. Tie second 6" length into 2" wide bow around first bow. Tack to base of one pigtail. Repeat with remaining lengths of ribbon.

LONG LOOSE HAIR

Materials needed:
   One skein "fluffy" acrylic yarn; matching thread
   Ribbon to match clothing

1. Transfer hairline from pattern to doll's head. Also draw a line across back of head; see Diagram 3.
2. For hair on back of head, use yarn without cutting it from skein. Starting with end of yarn at left side of head and ½" above hairline, make 4" loops, tacking yarn in place with matching thread; see Diagram 4. Continue until hairline is covered. Cut yarn end ½" above hairline at right side of head.
3. For bangs and hair on top of head, use yarn without cutting it from skein. Starting with end of yarn at left side of head and ¼" below hairline, make a 1" loop toward face for bangs, tacking in place with matching thread. Then make a 4" loop toward back of head, tacking in place with matching thread; see Diagram 5. Continue until hairline is

covered. Cut yarn end ¼" from hairline at right side of head.
4. Pull hair on top of head to back, covering attachment of hair on back of head. Wrap thread around hair and tie securely; see Diagram 6.

For **Rebecca**, cut six 6" lengths of ¼" wide satin ribbon. Tie each length into a 1½" wide bow. Tack three bows in one place to each side of head; see photo.

For **Megan**, roll bottom of hair up to neck and tack in place with matching thread; see Diagram 6.

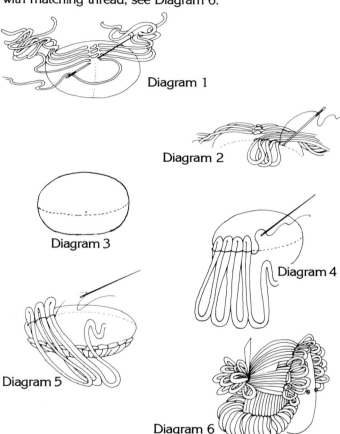

Diagram 1

Diagram 2

Diagram 3

Diagram 4

Diagram 5

Diagram 6

GENERAL INSTRUCTIONS FOR DOLL CLOTHES

SEAMS: All seams are ¼". In most cases, the seam should also be overcast with a zig-zag stitch.
BUTTONHOLES: Measure for all buttonholes to extend ⅛" beyond width of button. Mark placement with dressmaker's pen. Sew rectangle around mark with smallest machine stitch. (Most machine buttonhole stitching is too bulky.) Buttonholes may also be done by hand.
SKIRT LENGTHS: All dress and petticoat skirts should measure 6½" between waist seam and lower edge after hemming. Pinafore skirts are to be 4½" finished. If attaching trim

to bottom edge, compensate for ¼" seam allowance on skirt and trim. To add tucks to skirts, add twice the depth of each tuck to length of skirt.
GATHERS: To prepare fabric for gathering by machine, sew two parallel rows of long stitches ⅛" and ¼" from edge of fabric. Leave ends of thread 2" or 3" long. Pull two bobbin threads and gather to fit distance indicated. Long edges may need to be gathered from both ends. Disperse fullness evenly and secure in seam.
BODICE: All dress and petticoat bodices are fully lined, which hides most seams.

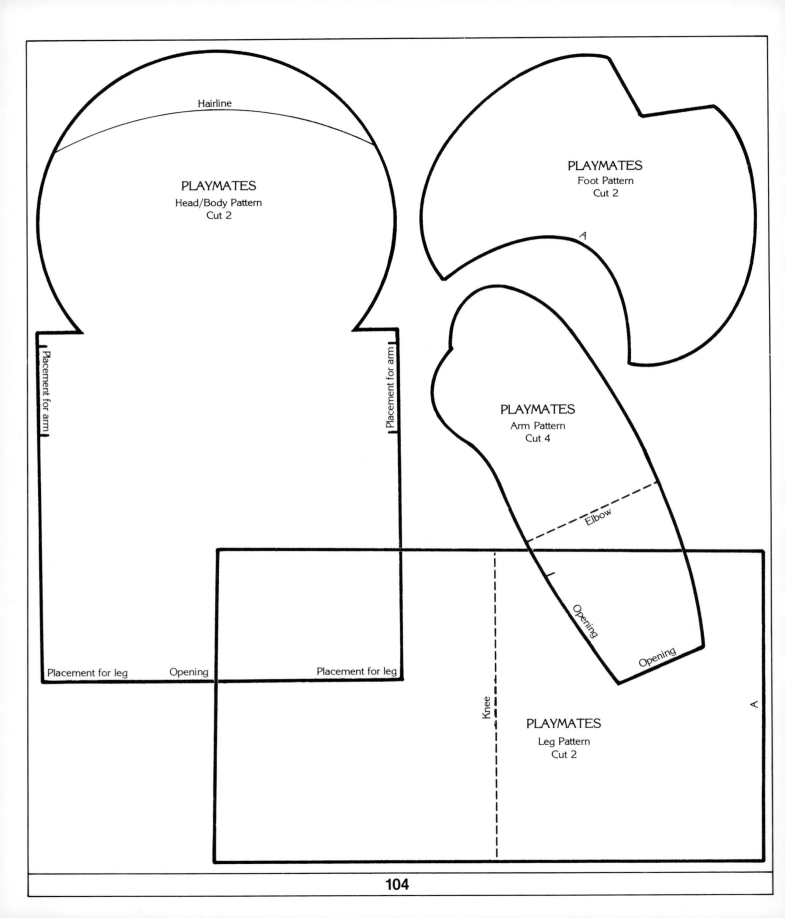

PLAYMATES
Head/Body Pattern
Cut 2

Hairline

Placement for arm

Placement for arm

Placement for leg

Opening

Placement for leg

PLAYMATES
Foot Pattern
Cut 2

A

PLAYMATES
Arm Pattern
Cut 4

Elbow

Opening

Opening

A

Knee

PLAYMATES
Leg Pattern
Cut 2

DOLL DRESS

Note: All seams are ¼".

Materials needed:

    ⅜ yd. 45" wide fabric; matching thread

    Two ⅛" wide white buttons

    Tracing paper for patterns

A. Prepare fabric:

  1. Make patterns for bodice front, bodice back, sleeve and collar, transferring all information.

  2. From fabric, cut one 8" x 30" piece for skirt and each pattern piece as indicated on patterns. Also cut two 1¼" x 3½" pieces for cuffs.

B. Construct dress:

  1. RIGHT sides together, stitch two collar pieces together. Trim seam allowance to ⅛". Turn; press. Repeat for second pair of collar pieces.

  2. RIGHT sides of two bodice back and one bodice front pieces together, stitch shoulders.

  3. Place collar pieces at neck of one bodice unit, matching pieces at center front. Stitch neckline; see Diagram 1.

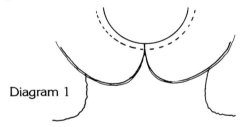

Diagram 1

  4. RIGHT sides of both bodice units together, match shoulder seams and center back opening. Stitch center back, around neck and center back. Trim corners, clip neckline and turn. Handle both bodice units as one.

  5. Mark centers of shoulder and wrist edges of sleeves; see pattern. Stitch gathering threads on shoulder and wrist edges.

  6. Mark center of one 3½" edge of wrist pieces. Match centers of cuff piece to center of wrist edge. Gather sleeve to 3½". Stitch sleeve to cuff piece. Repeat.

  7. RIGHT sides together, match center of shoulder edge to shoulder seam. Gather sleeve to fit; stitch. Repeat.

  8. Fold RIGHT sides of bodice/sleeve unit together. Stitch side seam, sleeve and ends of wrist piece. Repeat.

  9. Fold cuff double to WRONG side and slip stitch, covering raw edges.

  10. Fold RIGHT sides of skirt piece together. Stitch 5" of 8" edge; backstitch. Fold edges of 3" opening double to WRONG side and stitch narrow hem, see Diagram 2.

ELIZABETH

Barefooted, with brown hair in pigtails tied in three colors of ribbon, Elizabeth wears three layers of calico. Her pinafore with its ruffled shoulders is a grape-colored print, her dress is a plum-colored print, and her pantaloons are made from a plum-on-cream print.

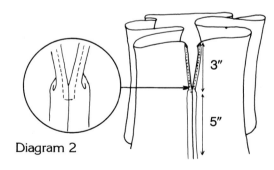

Diagram 2

  11. Mark center of 30" edge with opening. Stitch gathering threads around edge with opening. RIGHT sides together, match center of gathered edge to center of bottom edge of bodice front. Gather skirt to fit bodice; stitch. Zig-zag over raw edges.

  12. Fold 1½" of bottom edge of skirt to WRONG side. Fold raw edge under ¼". Slip stitch hem.

  13. Mark placement for two buttonholes on bodice back. Make buttonholes. Sew two buttons on opposite edge edge of bodice back.

MEGAN

A red-head wearing blue slippers, Megan is dressed for a party. Her white woven stripe pinafore is trimmed in 1½" wide white eyelet and is worn over a blue with white window pane checked dress with the reverse color pattern in the collar. Her petticoat fabric is white with blue stripe and has blue buttonhole stitching around the neck, armholes, and waist. The doll's pantaloons are white with blue check fabric and blue buttonhole stitching was added to the folded edge around the ankles.

PETTICOAT

Note: All seams are ¼".

Materials needed:
   ¼ yd. 45" fabric; matching thread
   Two ⅛" wide snaps
   ⅞ yd. ½" wide eyelet trim
   Tracing paper for patterns

A. Prepare fabric:
   1. Make patterns for dress bodice front and dress bodice back, transferring all information.
   2. From fabric, cut one 7" x 30" piece for skirt. To adjust for trim, see General Instructions. Also cut bodice pieces as indicated on patterns.
B. Construct petticoat:
   1. Complete Steps B2 and B4 of Doll Dress but do not turn bodice.
   2. Stitch armholes but not sides. Turn bodice by bringing back halves through layers of bodice front.
   3. RIGHT sides together, stitch sides of bodice.

4. Complete Steps B10, stitching 3" of 6" edge, and B11 of Doll Dress.
5. Measure width of eyelet trim and petticoat skirt from waist seam to lower edge. Allowing for ¼" seam, trim lower edge of petticoat so finished length is 6½".
6. RIGHT sides together, stitch eyelet to lower edge of petticoat.
7. Mark placement for snaps at center back of bodice where buttons are indicated on pattern. Sew on snaps.

PANTALOONS

Note: All seams are ¼".

Materials needed:
   ¼ yd. 45" fabric; matching thread
   14" of ⅛" elastic
   Tracing paper for patterns

A. Prepare fabric:
   1. Make pattern for pantaloons, transferring all information.
   2. From fabric, cut two pantaloon pieces.
B. Construct pantaloons:
   1. RIGHT sides together, stitch center front and center back seams.
   2. To make casing, fold ⅝" to WRONG side on waist edge. Fold raw edge ⅛" under; stitch close to fold leaving ¾" opening. Also stitch close to fold at waist edge.
   3. RIGHT sides together, stitch legs.
   4. Fold 1" to WRONG side on ankle edge. Fold raw edge ⅛" under; stitch close to fold leaving ¾" opening. Also stitch parallel to and ¼" below first row of stitching to make casing. Repeat.
   5. Cut elastic into one 7" and two 3½" lengths. Thread elastic into casings with small safety pin. Secure ends together, overlapping ¼". Complete stitching on casings.

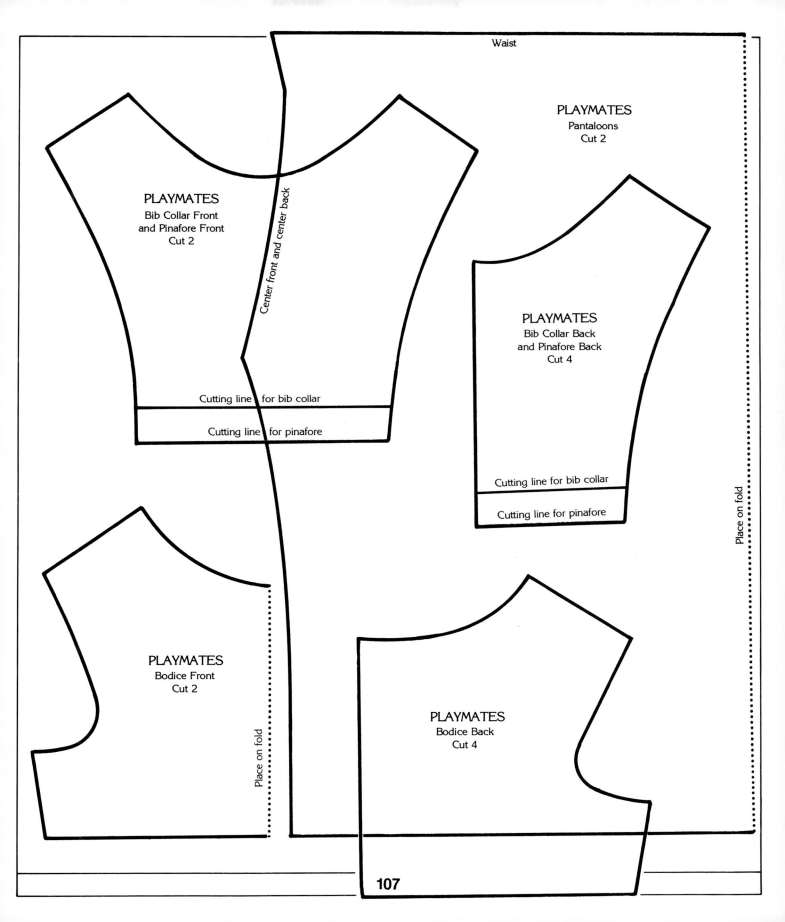

Waist

PLAYMATES
Pantaloons
Cut 2

PLAYMATES
Bib Collar Front
and Pinafore Front
Cut 2

Center front and center back

Cutting line for bib collar

Cutting line for pinafore

PLAYMATES
Bib Collar Back
and Pinafore Back
Cut 4

Cutting line for bib collar

Cutting line for pinafore

Place on fold

PLAYMATES
Bodice Front
Cut 2

Place on fold

PLAYMATES
Bodice Back
Cut 4

AMANDA

Amanda, barefoot and wearing a red gingham dress under her blue calico pinafore, is most comfortable in the country. Her blonde braids are tied with ribbon and tacked to the top of her head. Her pantaloons and petticoat are white eyelet fabric with 2" wide gathered eyelet on the petticoat hem.

PINAFORE

Materials needed:

    ¼ yd. 45" fabric; matching thread
    Optional: 1½ yds. 1½" wide white eyelet trim
    One hook and eye
    Tracing paper for patterns

A. Prepare fabric:
    1. Make patterns for pinafore front and pinafore back.
    2. From fabric, cut one 6" x 30" piece for skirt, one 1" x 30" piece for tie, two pinafore fronts and four pinafore backs.
    3. OPTION for ruffle on shoulders: cut one 2½" x 12" piece.

B. Construct pinafore:
    1. RIGHT sides together, stitch two back pieces to front piece at shoulders. Repeat for lining.
    2. OPTION for eyelet trim on ruffle: a) Cut two 12" lengths of eyelet trim. Stitch gathering threads on raw edge. Gather to 6". Raw edges together, stitch eyelet to outside edge of front and back of pinafore bodice; see Diagram 1. Repeat for second edge. b) Fold ruffle

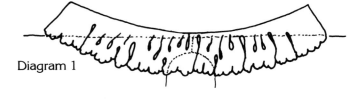

Diagram 1

pieces to measure 1¼" x 12". Stitch gathering threads through both layers on raw edge. Gather to 6". Match center of raw edge of ruffle to raw edge of pinafore bodice at shoulder. Taper ruffle and stitch to outside edge of front and back of pinafore bodice; see Diagram 2. Repeat for second edge.

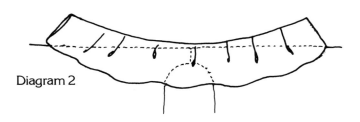

Diagram 2

    3. RIGHT sides of pinafore bodice and lining together, stitch center back, around neck and remaining center back. For pinafore without eyelet or ruffle, stitch outside edges of bodice. Turn by passing bodice backs through shoulders toward bodice front. For pinafore with eyelet or ruffle, turn and fold under outside edge of lining and slip stitch to bodice.

4. Stitch narrow hem on both 6" ends of skirt piece.
5. OPTION: Attach eyelet trim to one 30" edge of skirt piece.
6. Mark center of one 30" edge of skirt. Stitch gathering threads on that edge; gather to 7".
7. Mark center of 30" edges of tie. Also mark 3½" either side of center. RIGHT sides together, match tie and skirt at center marks. Match 6" ends to marks either side of center. Stitch tie to skirt; back stitch. See Diagram 3.

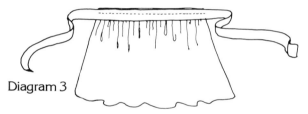

Diagram 3

8. Place lining side of bodice to WRONG side of skirt matching centers on raw edges. Also match center back edges of bodice to short ends of skirt. Stitch on stitching line of tie; see Diagram 4.

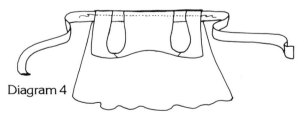

Diagram 4

9. Stitch narrow hem in one edge of loose ends of tie. Fold end with WRONG side together at 45 degree angle; see Diagram 5. Stitch narrow hem in remaining edge, securing fold.

Diagram 5

10. Fold center section of tie double, covering all raw edges; slip stitch. Fold bodice upright. Tack bodice edges to tie.
11. Fold hem 1" to WRONG side along lower edge of skirt. Fold raw edge under ¼"; slip stitch.
12. Attach hook and eye to neck edge of bodice at center back.

Option: Cut ½ yd. ¼" wide ribbon into three 6" lengths. Fold one length in half. Tack fold to center front of pinafore just below waistband. Repeat with remaining lengths, placing each ½" from either side of center ribbon. Trim ends at various lengths; see photo. Tie knot ½" from ribbon ends.

BIB COLLAR

Note: All seams are ¼".

Materials needed:
⅛ yd. 45" fabric to match dress; matching thread
1 yd. ¼" wide white lace
One hook and eye
Tracing paper for patterns

1. Make pattern for bib collar back and bib collar front.
2. From fabric, cut two bib collar front pieces and four bib collar back pieces.
3. RIGHT sides together, stitch shoulders of one bib collar front piece to two bib collar back pieces. Repeat with remaining front and back pieces.
4. RIGHT sides together, stitch bib collar pieces, leaving front bottom edge open. Clip corners. Turn; slip stitch opening closed.
5. Beginning at center back edge of collar, pin lace to lining side of collar around entire edge, allowing extra fullness at corners; see photo. Trim end; slip stitch. Stitch hook and eye to lining side of back of collar.

ANNIE

Annie, in her long blonde braids, sports blue chambray overalls with pockets and patches. Her pink gingham shirt buttons down the front.

OVERALLS

Note: All seams are ¼". All topstitching is with navy thread.

Materials needed:
    ¼ yd. 45" blue chambray fabric; navy thread
    Two ⅛" wide white buttons
    Small piece pink gingham fabric for cuffs
    Tracing paper for patterns

A. Prepare fabric:
    1. Make pattern for overalls, transferring all information. Also make pattern for side pockets.
    2. From blue fabric, cut two overall pieces.
    3. Measure 2½" from top edge of bib and cut pattern horizontally to make pattern for bib lining. Cut two bib lining pieces.
    4. Also cut two 2" x 1¾" pieces for bib pocket, two side pocket pieces and two 1" x 9" pieces for straps.
    5. From pink gingham fabric, cut two 4½" x 2" pieces for cuffs.

B. Construct overalls:
    1. Fold long raw edges of one strap piece ¼" to WRONG side. Fold folded edges together to make strap ¼" x 9". Topstitch close to both long folds. Repeat. Set aside.
    2. RIGHT sides of two bib pocket pieces together, stitch, leaving 1" opening. Trim corners; turn. Topstitch one 1½" edge. Set aside.
    3. RIGHT sides together, stitch center front and center back seams of overall pieces and bib lining pieces.
    4. Place bib pocket on overalls front as indicated on pattern with topstitched edge at top. Topstitch remaining three sides, folding edges inside at 1" opening.
    5. Fold bottom edge of bib lining ¼" to WRONG side; stitch.
    6. Pin one end of each strap to bib back ¼" from corner and with raw edges matching; see Diagram 1.

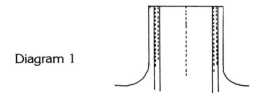

Diagram 1

    7. RIGHT sides of overalls and bib lining together, match at center front and center back seams. Stitch entire top edge of overalls. Clip curved seams and trim corners; turn and press. Topstitch top edge of overalls.
    8. Place side pockets on overalls front as indicated on pattern. Fold under ¼" on all sides; topstitch all sides. (Pockets do not open.)
    9. Topstitch knees on overalls front as indicated on pattern.
    10. RIGHT sides together, stitch legs; turn.
    11. Fold RIGHT sides of one cuff piece together to measure 2¼" x 2". Stitch 2" ends. Repeat.
    12. Fold again with WRONG sides together and raw edges matching. Match raw edges and seam in gingham cuff to WRONG side of leg seam; stitch. Turn cuff to RIGHT side of leg. Tack on seams. Repeat.
    13. Make buttonholes as shown on pattern. Sew buttons ¾" from end of straps.

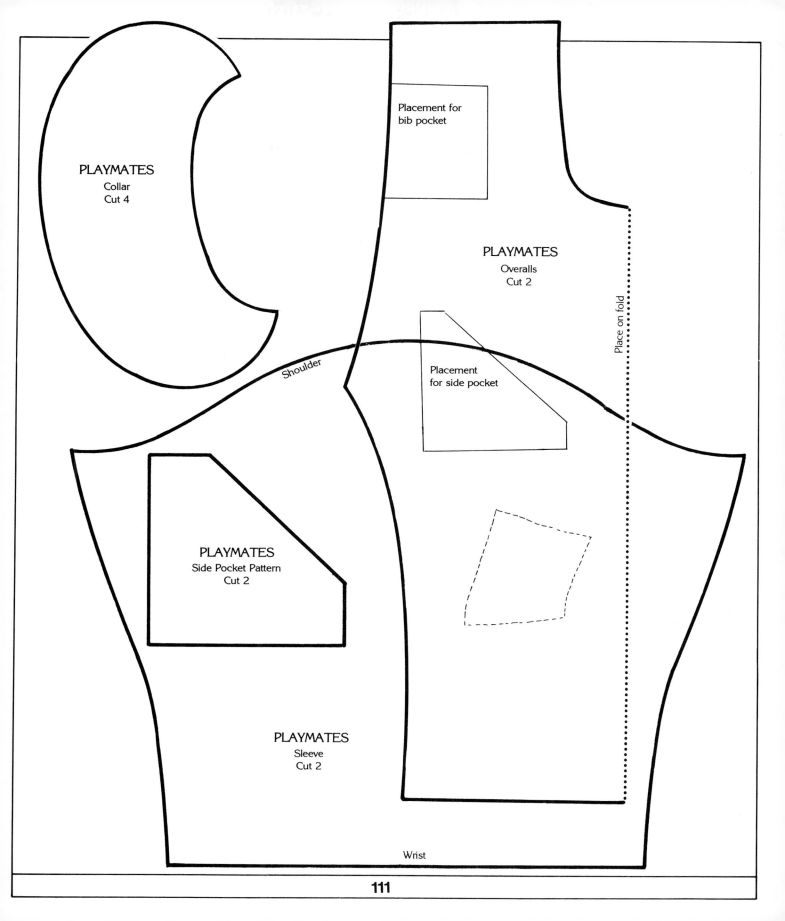

PLAYMATES
Collar
Cut 4

Placement for
bib pocket

PLAYMATES
Overalls
Cut 2

Place on fold

Shoulder

Placement
for side pocket

PLAYMATES
Side Pocket Pattern
Cut 2

PLAYMATES
Sleeve
Cut 2

Wrist

CATHERINE

In her Christmas print dress, Catherine is dressed for a holiday. The green pinafore she wears has optional ribbon trim and it matches her green painted shoes. Her pantaloons and petticoat are made of white dotted Swiss fabric and the petticoat hem is trimmed with ¾" wide flat eyelet. Catherine's dark brown hair is tied with ribbons into pigtails.

SHIRT

Note: All seams are ¼".

Materials needed:
 ¼ yd. 45" wide 1/16" pink gingham; white thread
 Three ⅛" wide white buttons
 Tracing paper for patterns

A. Prepare fabric:
   1. Make patterns for bodice front and bodice back, extending lower edge of each piece 1½". Label patterns: bodice front becomes shirt back; bodice back becomes shirt front.
   2. Also make patterns for collar and sleeve.
   3. From pink gingham fabric, cut one shirt back, two shirt fronts, four collars and two sleeves. Also cut two 3½" x 1½" wrist bands and 1" wide bias strip 9" long.

B. Construct shirt:
   1. RIGHT sides together, stitch two collar pieces, leaving neckline edge open. Trim seam allowance to ⅛". Turn; press. Repeat. Topstitch outside edge close to seam.
   2. RIGHT sides together, stitch shirt fronts to back at shoulders.
   3. To make front band, fold center front edge ½" to RIGHT side of fabric. Fold edge under ⅛"; see Diagram 1. Repeat.

Diagram 1   Diagram 2

   4. Topstitch both folded edges close to folds; see Diagram 2.
   5. Mark center back of neckline. Match collar pieces to RIGHT side of shirt on either side of mark; stitch.
   6. RIGHT sides together match bias to neck, folding ¼" to WRONG sides at ends; stitch. Clip curved seam. Fold bias double to WRONG side of shirt and slip stitch.
   7. Complete Steps B5 through B9 of Doll Dress.
   8. Fold ¼" double to WRONG side around bottom of shirt; stitch hem.
   9. Mark placement for three vertical buttonholes ½" apart on front band of shirt. Make buttonholes. Sew three buttons on opposite front band.

HAT

Materials needed:
    4" wide straw hat (available at craft supply store)
    13" of ¼" wide white flat lace
    Small pieces ⅛" wide pink and green ribbon
    White glue

    1. Glue lace to edge of hat.
    2. Tie knots in ribbon. Cut apart close to knots. Glue
       knots to hat.

SHOES

Materials needed:
    Acrylic paint in color to match clothing
    Small paint brush
    Two ⅛" wide white buttons (optional)
    Dressmaker's pen

1. Mark top edge of shoes and straps with dressmaker's pen
   on doll body; see Diagram 1.

Diagram 1

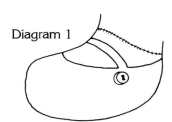

2. Paint shoes. Allow to dry thoroughly.
3. Sew buttons on outside; see Diagram 1.

REBECCA

Rebecca is wearing a pink print dress with a white bib collar and cuffs. A ⅛" deep tuck is parallel to and 1" above the hem of the dress. The trim on the bib is ¼" wide flat white lace and ¾" wide flat white lace is attached to the tuck. Her petticoat is white batiste with ¼" wide flat white lace at the neck and hem and has three ⅛" deep tucks parallel to the hem of the petticoat. Her pantaloons are also white batiste. The blue sash is 30" of ½" wide picot edge satin ribbon. Rebecca's hair is blonde and the top is pulled into a bun at the back of her head. Her shoes have a strap and small button and are painted light blue.

only the very best of what
is good enough for

Good friends

Cover sample: Stitched on White Aida 14. Finished design size is 10⅜" x 7¼". Cut fabric 17" x 14". Finished design sizes using other fabrics are — Aida 11: 13¼" x 9¼"; Aida 18: 8" x 5⅝"; Hardanger 22: 6½" x 4⅝".

you have to give a friend

BATES		DMC	(used for cover sample)
			Step One: Cross-stitch (two strands)
301		744	Yellow · pale
49		963	Dusty Rose · vy. lt.
49		3689	Mauve · lt.
69		3687	Mauve
95		554	Violet · lt.
99		552	Violet · dk.
975		775	Baby Blue · lt.
158		747	Sky Blue · vy. lt.
167		598	Turquoise · lt.
145		334	Baby Blue · med.
208		563	Jade · lt.
885		739	Tan · ultra vy. lt.
882		407	Sportsman Flesh · dk.
380		839	Beige Brown · dk.
397		762	Pearl Gray · vy. lt.
398		415	Pearl Gray
			Step Two: Back Stitch (one strand)
382		3371	Black Brown
			Step Three: French Knots (one strand)
382		3371	Black Brown

My paper doll

Cover sample for **picture**: Stitched on Cream Aida 14. Finished design size is 14¾" x 11¼". Cut fabric 21" x 17". Finished design sizes using other fabrics are — Aida 11: 18¾" x 14¼"; Aida 18: 11½" x 8¾"; Hardanger 22: 9⅜" x 7⅛".

Also needed: ⅜ yd. ⅛" wide blue satin ribbon
Three ¼" wide white flat buttons
One ¼" wide red flat button

Cover sample for **paper doll and clothing:** Stitched on Cream Perforated Paper 15. Finished design size for doll is 5⅞" x 7½". Use one 9" x 12" piece Perforated Paper for doll. Small pieces Perforated Paper may be used for clothing. Complete cross-stitch. Use color pencils to fill in as indicated in code below.

Also needed:
⅜ yd. ⅛" wide blue satin ribbon for bows in hair and on blue pinafore
Five ¼" wide white flat buttons for green jacket and blue pinafore
One ¼" wide red flat button
Rubber cement

Finishing instructions for paper doll and clothing: With rubber cement, glue doll and clothing to manila paper. Cut ⅛" from back stitching. Make paper doll stand from manila paper; see photo.

DMC			(used for cover sample)
			Step One: Cross-stitch (two strands)
1	–		White
926	· /		Ecru
297	J	743	Yellow · med.
347	T	945	Sportsman Flesh
893	N	224	Shell Pink · lt.
24	O	776	Pink · med.
19	♥	817	Coral Red · vy. dk.
44	a ◢	816	Garnet
209	Z	913	Nile Green · med.
229	■	700	Christmas Green · bright
159	U	3325	Baby Blue
145	X	334	Baby Blue · med.
147	S ◢	312	Navy Blue · lt.
149	H	336	Navy Blue
379	E	840	Beige Brown · med.
380	△	838	Beige Brown · vy. dk.
			Step Two: Back Stitch (one strand)
297		743	Yellow · med. (blue dress on doll)
149		336	Navy Blue (all else)
			Step Three: French Knots (one strand)
403	●	310	Black
			Step Four: Buttons
	■		White ¼" wide flat buttons
	■		Red ¼" wide flat button
			Step Five: Bows
	K		Three small bows tied with blue ribbon for doll's hair and blue pinafore; see photo.

BATES		DMC		(used for cover sample)
				Step One: Cross-stitch (two strands)/Colored Pencils
	–			White
	· /			Unstitched perforated paper
297	J	743		Yellow · med.
	T			Pink colored pencil
	N			Red colored pencil
	O			Red colored pencil
19	♥	817		Coral Red · vy. dk.
44	a ◢	816		Garnet
	Z			Green colored pencil
229	■	700		Christmas Green · bright
	U			Blue colored pencil
	X			Blue colored pencil
147	S ◢	312		Navy Blue · lt.
149	H	336		Navy Blue
379	E	840		Beige Brown · med.
380	△	838		Beige Brown · vy. dk.
				Step Two: Back stitch (one strand)
297		743		Yellow · med. (blue dress on doll)
149		336		Navy Blue (all else)
				Step Three: French Knots
	●			Black felt tip pen
				Step Four: Buttons
	■			White ¼" wide flat buttons
	■			Red ¼" wide flat button
				Step Five: Bows
	K			Two small bows tied with blue ribbon for doll's hair; see photo.
				One small bow tied with blue ribbon for blue pinafore; see photo.

Opposite page: My Paper Doll is a timeless treasure, whether cross-stitched, framed and hung on the wall or finished on perforated paper and ready for play.

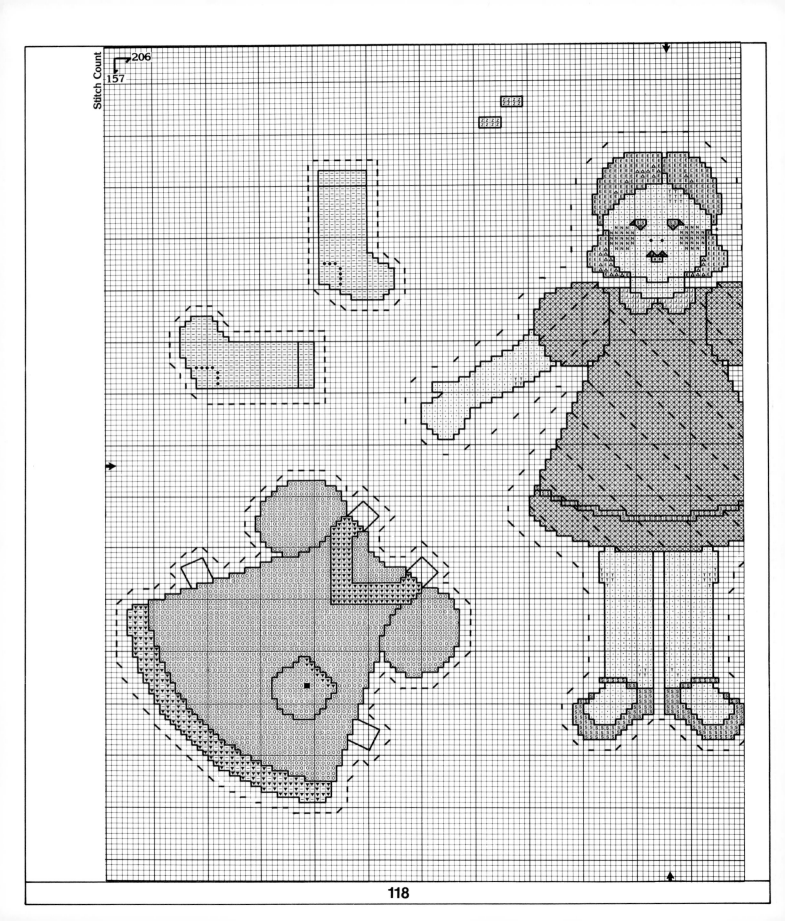

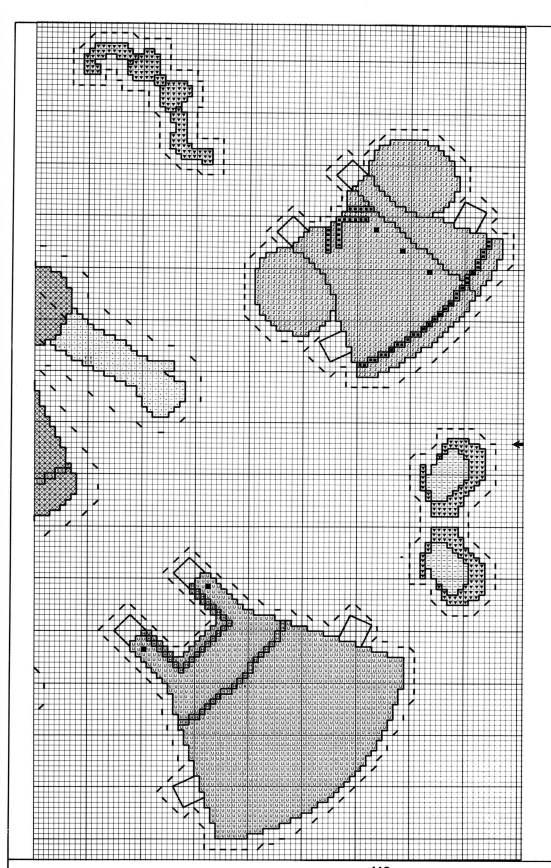

My paper doll

September

September's child is rosy of cheek,
Tumbling and gay, with adventure to seek.
With candied apples and a little stuffed bear,
Hand-in-hand, they go to the fair.

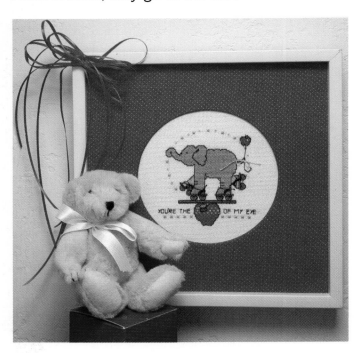

Have you ever seen a Roller Skating Elephant? Maybe not. This one, balanced on an apple, will charm the child in all of us.

Opposite page: Saturday at the fair! In the arena the Juggling Bears and the Bean Bag Doll prepare their act. In the second show, the Roller Skating Elephant and Swinging Bear are the featured attractions. Join us for Apples, Apples, Apples or Ice Cream Cones after the show.

Ice cream cones

Materials needed for one cone:

Completed cross-stitch on Herta for cone; matching thread
6½" x 6½" piece fabric for ice cream; matching thread
7" of narrow lace or eyelet
12" of ⅛" wide ribbon
6" x 6" polyester fleece
Medium weight fusible interfacing
Stuffing
2" styrofoam ball
White glue
Tracing paper for patterns

A. Prepare cone:
  1. Trim Herta to ¾" outside stitched area. Fuse interfacing to WRONG side of design piece. Trim to ⅛" of stitched area. Handle carefully to avoid raveling.
  2. Roll design piece, RIGHT side out, to form cone with cross-stitching just meeting at seam. Slip stitch seam, beginning at bottom of cone.
  3. Apply small amount of glue to bottom of cone to control raveling.
  4. Fill cone moderately with stuffing.

B. Prepare ice cream:
  1. Make patterns for 6½" and 6" circles; see General Instructions.
  2. From fabric for ice cream, cut one 6½" circle; stitch gathering thread ¼" from edge. From fleece, cut one 6" circle.
  3. Place styrofoam ball, covered with fleece, next to WRONG side of fabric and pull gathering thread so fabric fits tightly; secure thread.
  4. Place ice cream on top of cone with gathered edges next to stuffing. Slip stitch together.
  5. Using lace, eyelet and/or ribbon, slip stitch trim to cone top to cover seam. If cones are to be used as ornaments, attach small loop of gold cord to cone at top of seam.

Cover sample: Stitched on Cream Herta 6. Finished design size is 3⅞" x 3⅞". Cut fabric 7" x 7". Finished design sizes using other fabrics are - Aida 11: 2⅛" x 2⅛"; Aida 14: 1⅝" x 1⅝"; Aida 18: 1¼" x 1¼"; Hardanger 22: 1" x 1".

BATES	DMC (used for cover sample)
	Step One: Cross-stitch (four strands)
363	463 Tan

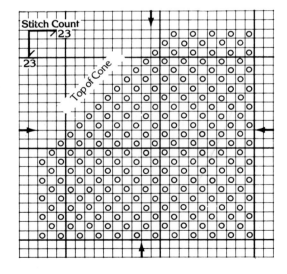

Stitch Count
23
23
Top of Cone

Swinging bear

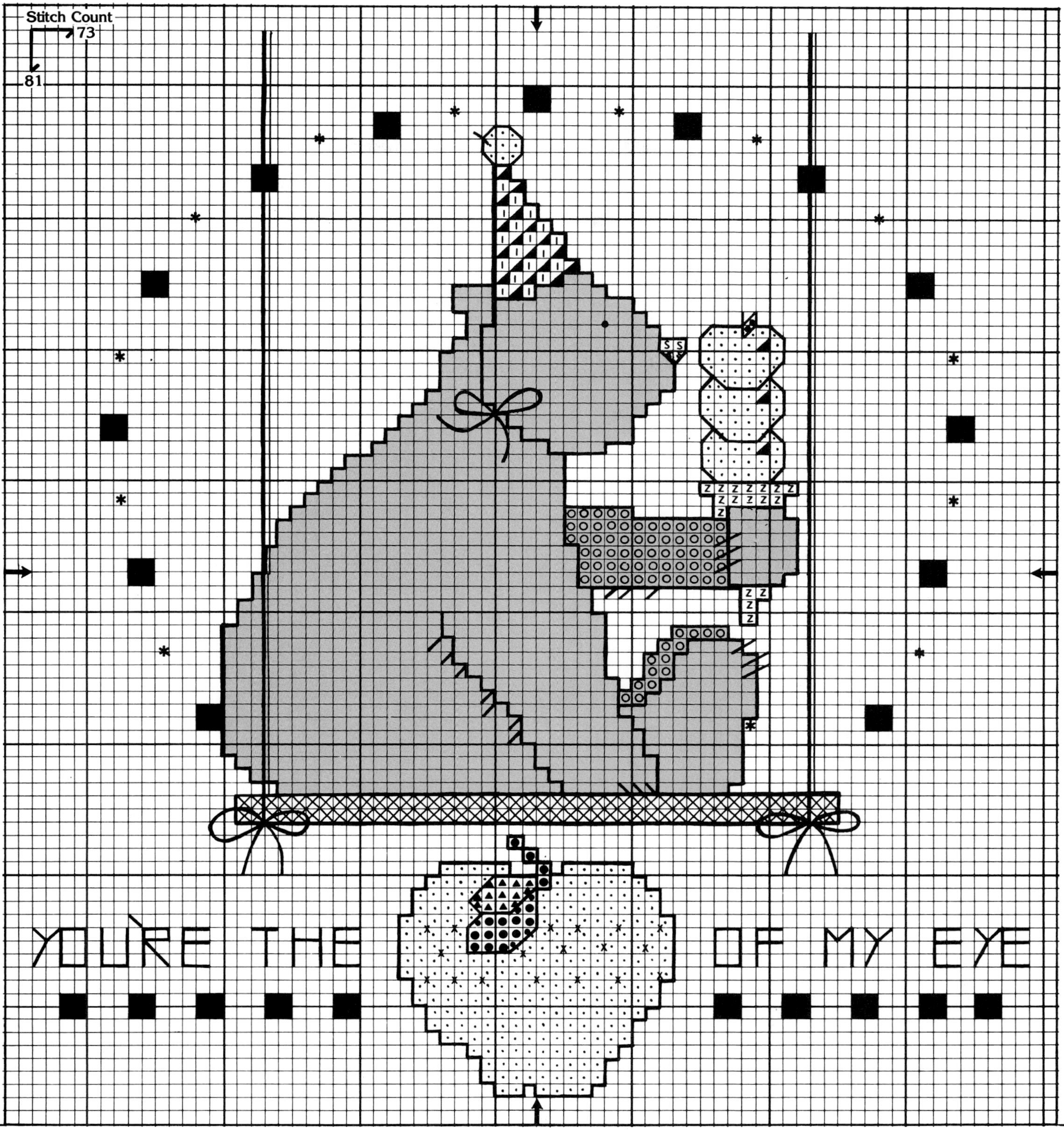

Stitch Count
73
81

YOU'RE THE ♥ OF MY EYE

123

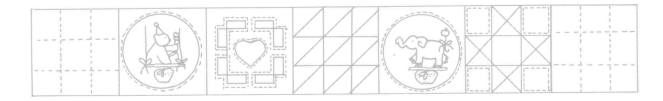

Swinging bear

Cover sample: Stitched on White Aida 18. Finished design size is 4" x 4½". Cut fabric 10" x 11". Finished design sizes using other fabrics are — Aida 11: 6⅝" x 7⅜"; Aida 14: 5¼" x 5¾"; Hardanger 22: 3⅜" x 3⅝".

BATES		DMC	(used for cover sample)
			Step One: Cross-stitch (two strands)
1	◢		White
291	z	444	Lemon · dk.
27	ı	893	Carnation · lt.
46	· ◿	666	Christmas Red · bright
978	✕	322	Navy Blue · vy. lt.
238	▲ ◢	703	Chartreuse
229	● ◢	700	Christmas Green · bright
363	o	436	Tan
309	▨ ◿	435	Brown · vy. lt.
403	s ◢	310	Black
			Step Two: Back Stitch (one strand)
403	⌐	310	Black
			Step Three: French Knots (one strand)
403	●	310	Black
			Step Four: Smyrna Cross (two strand)
159	■	3325	Baby Blue
			Step Five: Bead Work
	x		Crystal
	*		Light Blue
			Step Six: Long Loose Stitch (one strand)
	❘		Black Pearl Cotton #8 (swing ropes)
			Step Seven: Bows (one strand)
403	✿	310	Black floss · Bow Around Bear's Neck
		310	Black Pearl Cotton #8 · Bows On Swing

Roller skating elephant

Cover sample: Stitched on White Aida 18. Finished design size is 3⅞" x 4¼". Cut fabric 11" x 12". Finished design sizes using other fabrics are — Aida 11: 6⅜" x 7"; Aida 14: 5" x 5½"; Hardanger 22: 3⅛" x 3½".

BATES		DMC	(used for cover sample)
			Step One: Cross-stitch (two strands)
1	◢		White
27	ı ◿	893	Carnation · lt.
46	· ◿	666	Christmas Red · bright
978	✕	322	Navy Blue · vy. lt.
238	▲ ◢	703	Chartreuse
229	● ◢	700	Christmas Green · bright
900	⫼ ◢	3024	Brown Gray · vy. lt.
8581	▨ ◿	3023	Brown Gray · lt.
			Step Two: Back Stitch (one strand)
403	⌐	310	Black
			Step Three: French Knots (one strand)
403	●	310	Black
			Step Four: Smyrna Cross (two strands)
159	■	3325	Baby Blue
			Step Five: Bead Work
	x		Crystal
	*		Light Blue
			Step Six: Long Loose Stitch (one strand)
403	❘	310	Black
			Step Seven: Bows
	✿	744	Yellow Pearl Cotton #8 · Bow Around Elephant's Tail.
	◥	310	Black floss · Bows for Skates

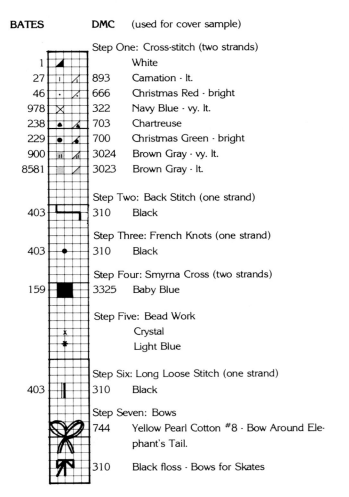

Roller skating elephant

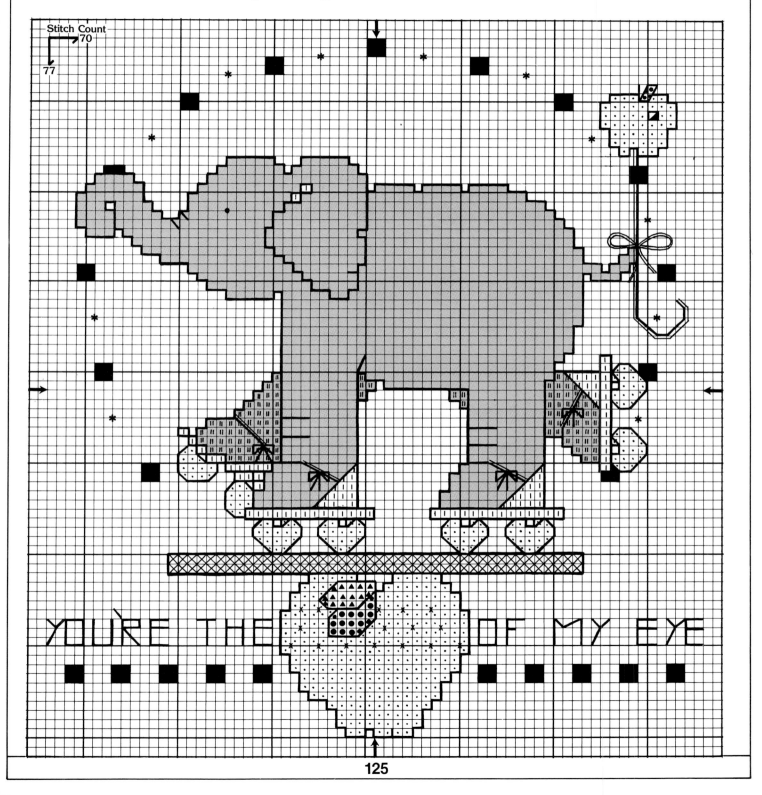

Stitch Count
70
77

YOU'RE THE ⬤⬤ OF MY EYE

Bean bag doll

Materials needed:
- ⅜ yd. 45" red/white check print fabric
- 5" x 5" piece white fabric; matching thread
- 3" x 5" piece yellow/white gingham fabric; yellow thread
- Two 1" x 1" pieces red/white pin dot fabric
- 5" of ¼" wide elastic
- Red thread
- Green thread
- 1 yd. white heavy craft yarn; large needle
- 1½ cups rice or popcorn
- Fusing material
- Tracing paper for patterns

A. Prepare fabric:
1. Make pattern for entire doll, following outside line on pattern and disregarding facial details. Also make patterns for entire circle for face, hair, and cheeks..
2. From red/white check fabric, cut two body pieces.
3. From white fabric, cut face.
4. From yellow/white gingham fabric, cut hair, transferring quilting lines to fabric.
5. From red/white pin dot fabric, cut two cheeks.
6. From fusing material, cut face and cheeks.
7. Cut elastic into four 1¼" pieces.

B. Construct doll:
1. Pin hair to face; do not fuse. With fusing material between face and body, fuse according to manufacturer's instructions.
2. With yellow thread, top stitch lines in hair as indicated on pattern. Using double strand of yarn in large needle, thread under yellow fabric (hair) between stitching lines. Clip yarn ends close to fabric. With yellow thread and wide satin stitch, machine applique lower edge of hair, catching ends of yarn in stitching. Satin stitch around outside edge of hair and entire face.
3. With green thread and narrow satin stitch, machine applique around cheeks.

Bright apple cheeks adorn the Bean Bag Doll, a project made entirely by machine.

4. With green thread and narrow satin stitch, sew stems of "apple" cheeks, eyes and buttons on body front as indicated on pattern.
5. Pin 1¼" pieces of elastic on WRONG side of each arm as indicated on pattern. Stretch elastic the width of fabric and zig-zag with white thread.
6. Place WRONG sides of body pieces together. With white thread and wide satin stitch, sew around entire outside edge of face next to yellow satin stitching, leaving 1" opening on one side. Fill with ½ cup rice or popcorn, adjusting amount as desired. Satin stitch opening closed.
7. With white thread and wide satin stitch, sew around entire body, leaving 1" opening on one shoulder. Fill with 1 cup of popcorn, adjusting amount as desired. Satin stitch opening closed.

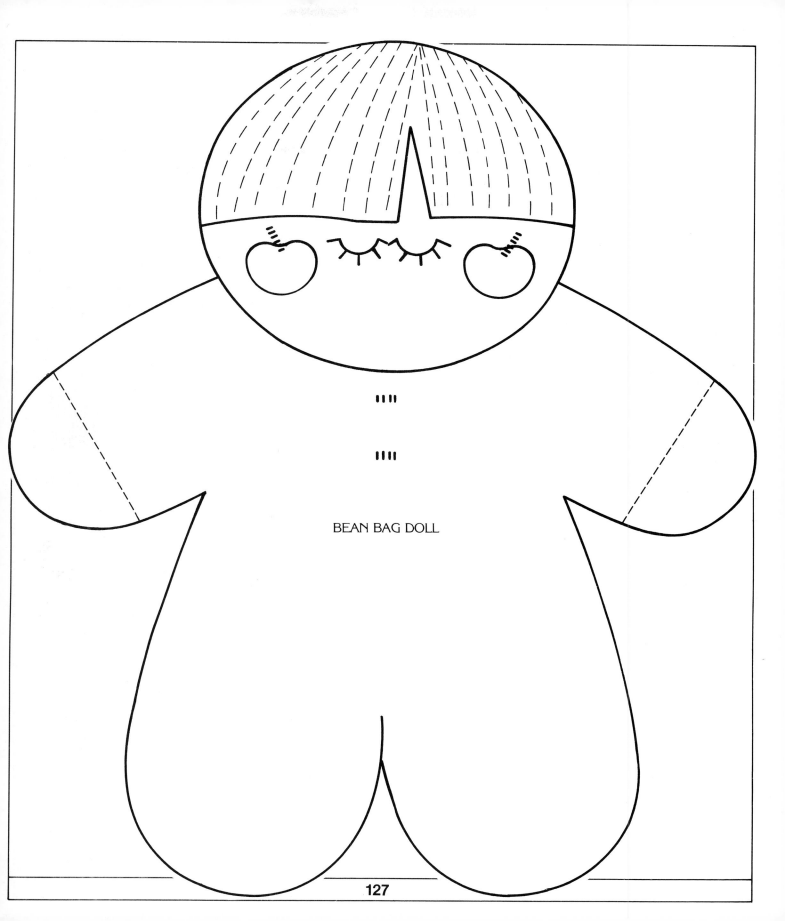

BEAN BAG DOLL

Apples, apples, apples
RATTLE

All seams are ⅜" except as noted.

Materials needed for one:
- ⅛ yd. red/white pin dot fabric; matching thread
- 5" x 15" piece green fabric for leaves and stem; matching thread
- Small pieces batting for leaves
- Stuffing
- Small, light weight cardboard box (approximately 1½" square)
- Three ½" jingle bells
- 2½" long needle
- Tracing paper for patterns

A. Prepare fabric:
  1. Make patterns for apple front/back, side and leaf.
  2. From red fabric, cut one apple side and two front/back pieces.
  3. From green fabric, cut leaves. Also cut one piece 2½" x 2½" for stem.
  4. From batting, cut two leaves.

B. Construct apple:
  1. RIGHT sides of apple side and apple front together, match center bottoms. Stitch from center bottom to center top; back stitch. Repeat for second half of front. Repeat stitching apple back to opposite edge of apple side.
  2. Stuff lower part of apple. Place bells inside box and place box in center of apple. Stuff firmly around box until apple is full.
  3. Fold under ½" seam allowance at center top opening. Using a double strand of thread, stitch gathering thread around top of apple close to folded edge. Pulling thread, gather fabric until area between sides is 1½" wide. Knot securely.
  4. Using long needle, secure a double strand of thread in center of gathered seam. Push needle into apple center, through cardboard box, and out center bottom. Make a single ¼" stitch; return needle through box and apple to center top. Pull on thread until desired fullness is achieved and secure thread.

C. Construct leaves:
  1. RIGHT sides of fabric leaf pieces together, place over batting leaf; pin. Stitch three pieces together, leaving 3" opening in one side. Clip corners and turn. Slip stitch opening closed. Repeat for second leaf.
  2. Machine stitch veins in leaves as indicated on pattern.

3. RIGHT sides together, fold stem piece in half and stitch one end and side with ¼" seam. Turn RIGHT side out and stuff lightly.
4. Position leaves as desired and tack in place on center top of apple. Tack underside of leaves to apple. Fold open end of stem under ¼" twice and stitch in place to center top of apple, covering ends of leaves.

Center Top

Seam Line

APPLE RATTLE
Side
Cut 1

Center Bottom
Place on Fold

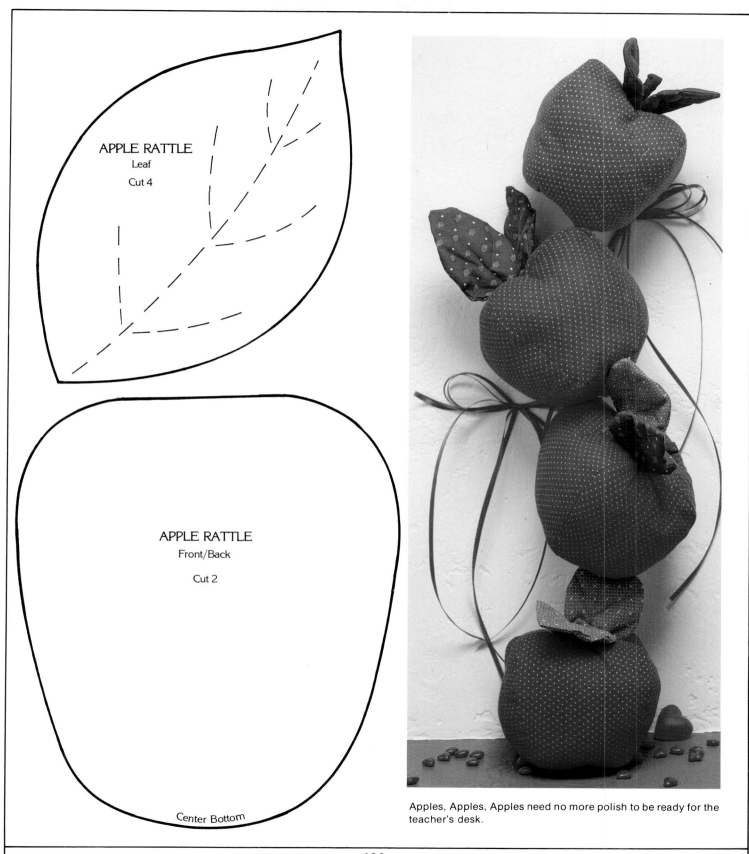

APPLE RATTLE
Leaf
Cut 4

APPLE RATTLE
Front/Back

Cut 2

Center Bottom

Apples, Apples, Apples need no more polish to be ready for the teacher's desk.

Juggling bears

Materials needed:

¼ yd. 45" tan/white pin dot fabric for bears; matching thread

⅛ yd. 45" blue/white dot fabric for hats and balls; matching thread

Small pieces red/white check print fabric for bears' cheeks

1 yd. 45" muslin; matching thread

2 yds. red/white pin dot fabric; matching thread

⅞ yd. tan/red stripe fabric; see Step A5

Fusing material

Navy thread

Batting

Dressmaker's pen

Tracing paper for patterns

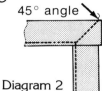

45° angle

Diagram 2

A. Prepare fabric:
1. Make patterns for bear, hat, apple, cheek, ball and stripe on ball.
2. From tan/white pin dot fabric, cut four bears, two facing left and two facing right.
3. From blue/white dot fabric, cut four hats and four balls. From red/white check fabric, cut four cheeks.
4. From muslin, cut one piece 34½" x 34½".
5. From red/white pin dot fabric, cut one piece 45" x 45" for back; four strips 5½" x 43" for border, four apples and four stripes on balls.
6. From tan/red stripe fabric, cut four strips 1⅜" x 27¼" for sashing. Extra fabric was needed for model because stripe is printed vertically. (If using a stripe which is printed horizontally on the bolt or any other fabric, purchase ¼ yd. and cut as indicated above.)
7. From fusing material, cut four each of the following: bears, hats, cheeks, apples, balls and stripes.

B. Construct quilt top:
1. With fusing material between fabric and muslin top, place bears in corners facing each other and with backs and bottoms 5¾" from edges; fuse according to manufacturer's instructions. Fuse hats, cheeks and apples to quilt top; see Diagram 1. Fuse balls to quilt top; see Diagram 1. Fuse stripes to balls.
2. With dressmaker's pen, transfer all markings for eyes, noses, apple sticks, stems and leaves, arms, legs, bow and pom-pom.
3. With tan thread and wide machine satin stitch, sew around each bear body and over lines for arm, hand, neck and leg. Satin stitch around cheeks with tan thread.
4. Satin stitch around balls with blue thread. Satin stitch around apples and stripes with red thread.

5. With navy thread, satin stitch hats, bows, sticks for apples, leaves, stems and bears' eyes, noses, claws and pom-poms.

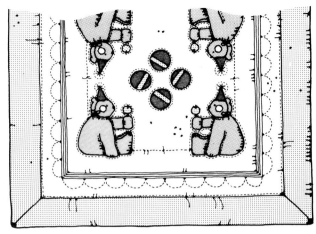

Diagram 1

C. Construct quilt:
1. Mark centers of each edge of muslin. Center striped sashing strips with WRONG side up 4" inside edges of muslin and stitch with ¼" seam. Fold sashing strips RIGHT side up. Press, turning under ¼" of second side. Fold corners to make 45-degree angle; slip stitch.
2. Mark centers of one 43" side of each strip of red/white pin dot. RIGHT sides together, match center of strip to center of side. Stitch with ½" seam to within ½" of muslin corners; back stitch. Repeat for each side.
3. To miter corners, fold RIGHT sides of red/white pin dot fabric together and stitch corner at 45-degree angle; see Diagram 2. Trim corner to ½" seam allowance; press. Repeat for each corner.
4. Place red/white pin dot fabric for backing WRONG side up on flat surface. Center batting over it; center quilt top over batting. Baste thoroughly.
5. By machine and using thread to match muslin, carefully quilt next to satin stitching around balls, then bears, hats and apples. Also quilt bears' arms and necks.
6. Quilt single line 3" inside striped pieces between bears' feet and on both edges of sashing.
7. Make pattern for quilted scallops by folding ball pattern in half. With dressmaker's pen, draw scallops along outside edge of striped pieces; see Diagram 1. Quilt on lines.
8. Quilt on muslin next to seam which joins red/white border.
9. Trim batting and back to match quilt top. Fold ½" seam allowance of both pieces inside and slip stitch around entire quilt.

October

Horses dance for October's child
Who loves the country and all that is wild.
Together they ride through tall autumn grass
Sharing the memories of days long past.

Stenciling, a craft which children love to learn, is used to make Two
Pink Sheep a versatile pillow.

Opposite page: A collection of friends from the country are gathered on the Barnyard Parade Quilt. Stars and hearts from Two Pink Sheep and A Pillow Pair scatter onto nearby Shirred Sachets. Old friends are kept close at heart in a Barnyard Friends Sampler.

Barnyard parade quilt

Materials needed:
- 1⅝ yds. 45" quilted double-sided cream muslin; matching thread
- 1 yd. 45" blue print fabric; matching thread
- ⅜ yd. 45" muslin
- ⅜ yd. 45" pink print fabric
- Rose, blue and white acrylic paints
- Dressmaker's pen
- Stenciling materials; see Stenciling Instructions

1. From quilted muslin, cut one 44" x 56" piece for quilt.
2. From blue print fabric, cut two 5½" x 44" pieces for panels and 2½" wide bias strips, piecing as needed, to equal 5¾ yds. for binding.
3. From muslin, cut two 5½" x 44" pieces for panels.
4. From pink print fabric, cut two 5½" x 44" pieces for panels.
5. Mark placement for pigs on pink print panel; see Diagram 1. Stencil seven rose pigs with marks on center of design and pig feet 1½" from bottom edge of panel. Repeat with second pink panel.

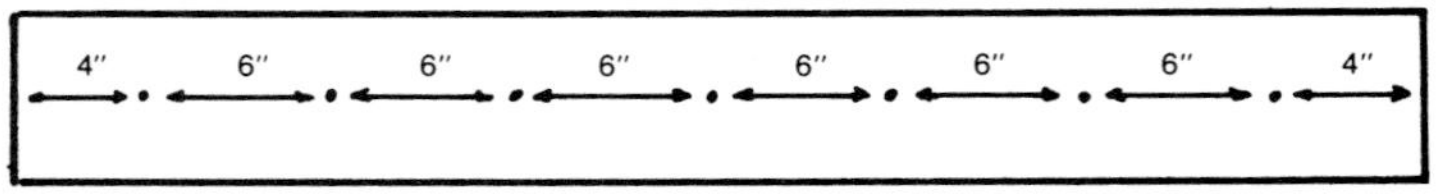

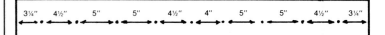

Diagram 1

6. Mark placement for stars and horses on muslin panel; see Diagram 2. Stencil stars with rose paint and horses with blue. Repeat with second muslin panel.

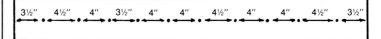

Diagram 2

7. Mark placement for sheep and hearts on blue print panel; see Diagram 3. Stencil hearts with rose paint and sheep with white. Designs painted with white may need two coats. Repeat with second print panel.

Diagram 3

8. With bottom of pig panel to top of horse panel and RIGHT sides together, stitch with ¼" seam. Repeat with bottom of horse panel to top of sheep panel. Press seams open. Repeat with remaining panels.
9. Draw lines with dressmaker's pen across both ends of quilt 20" from edge.
10. Match long raw edge of pink print panel to pen line. RIGHT sides together, with panels toward quilt center. Stitch ¼" from edge. Turn panels RIGHT side up. Baste panels to quilt top. Repeat with second set of panels.
11. Machine quilt as close as possible to seam line on both long seams. Repeat at opposite end.
12. Fold edge of blue print panel under ¼"; press. Top stitch edge to quilt top. Repeat at opposite end.
13. Round corners of quilt slightly. Pin 2½" wide bias strip to quilt edge with RIGHT sides together and raw edges matching, allowing extra fullness at corners. Stitch with ½" seam. Fold double to back and slip stitch.

Two pink sheep

Materials needed:
- 2⅜ yds. 45" lightweight blue print fabric; matching thread
- ¼ yd. 45" muslin; matching thread
- 2 yds. ⅛" wide cream grosgrain ribbon
- ¼ yd. fusing material
- 15" x 15" pillow form
- White and rose acrylic paints
- Stenciling materials; see Stenciling Instructions
- Dressmaker's pen
- Tracing paper for pattern

A. Prepare fabric:
1. Make stencil patterns for sheep and heart; see Stenciling Instructions.
2. Make pattern for 7½" circle; see General Instructions.
3. From print fabric, cut two 15" x 15" pieces for pillow front and back. Also cut 6" wide bias strips, piecing as needed, to equal 6 yds. for shirring and 4" wide bias strips, piecing as needed, to equal 3 yds. for ruffle.
4. From both muslin and fusing material, cut one circle like pattern.

B. Construct pillow:
  1. Mix rose and white paint to desired shade for darker sheep. Add white paint to half of mixture for lighter sheep.
  2. Stencil one sheep and three hearts on muslin circle with lighter pink paint. Stencil second sheep overlapping first sheep using darker pink paint.
  3. Center stenciled circle on RIGHT side of one 15" x 15" piece with fusing materials between fabrics; fuse according to manufacturer's directions. Using cream thread and wide satin stitch, machine applique entire edge of circle.
  4. Draw circle 1" outside edge of muslin circle using dressmaker's pen.
  5. RIGHT sides together, stitch ends of 6" wide bias strip to make one continuous piece. Stitch gathering threads along one raw edge. Gather to about 30". RIGHT sides together, place gathered edge on pen line of larger circle with shirring toward center. Stitch ½" from edge.
  6. Fold shirring RIGHT side out and baste to edges of pillow top, distributing fullness evenly. Trim to fit pillow top.
  7. RIGHT sides together, stitch ends of 4" wide bias strip to make one continuous piece. WRONG sides together, fold to measure 2" wide and press fold line. Fold bias strip into quarters and mark. Stitch gathering threads along raw edges through both layers.
  8. Round corners slightly. Pin quarter marks to corners of pillow top. Gather to fit pillow top. RIGHT sides together and matching all raw edges, stitch with ½" seam.
  9. RIGHT sides of pillow top and back together, match corners with ruffle folded toward center. Stitch top and back together with ½" seam, keeping ruffle smooth and leaving 8" opening. Turn. Insert pillow form. Slip stitch opening closed.
  10. Cut four 18" lengths of ribbon. Handling two lengths as one, tie 5" wide bow. Repeat with remaining ribbon. Tack bows to pillow; see photo.

Barnyard friends sampler

Cover sample: Stitched on White Linen 32 over two threads. Finished design size is 5¾" x 9". Cut fabric 12" x 15". Finished design sizes using other fabrics are — Aida 11: 8½" x 13⅛"; Aida 14: 6⅝" x 10¼"; Aida 18: 5⅛" x 8"; Hardanger 22: 4¼" x 6½".

BATES		DMC	(used for cover sample)

Step One: Cross-stitch (two strands)

BATES		DMC	
292	= ⁄	3078	Golden Yellow · vy. lt.
49	+ ⁄	963	Dusty Rose · vy. lt.
66	▨	3688	Mauve · med.
108	o ⁄	211	Lavender · lt.
95	X ⁄	554	Violet · lt.
98	● ⁄	553	Violet · med.
101	▲	327	Antique Violet · dk.
118	I	340	Blue Violet · med.
158	·	747	Sky Blue · vy. lt.
160	△ ⁄	813	Blue · lt.
978	o ⁄	322	Navy Blue · vy. lt.
131	X ⁄	798	Delft · dk.
185	∴	964	Seagreen · lt.
186	o	959	Seagreen · med.
187	●	958	Seagreen · dk.
942	▽	738	Tan · vy. lt.
363	+	436	Tan

Step Two: Back Stitch (one strand)

149	⌐	311	Navy Blue · med.

Barnyard friends sampler

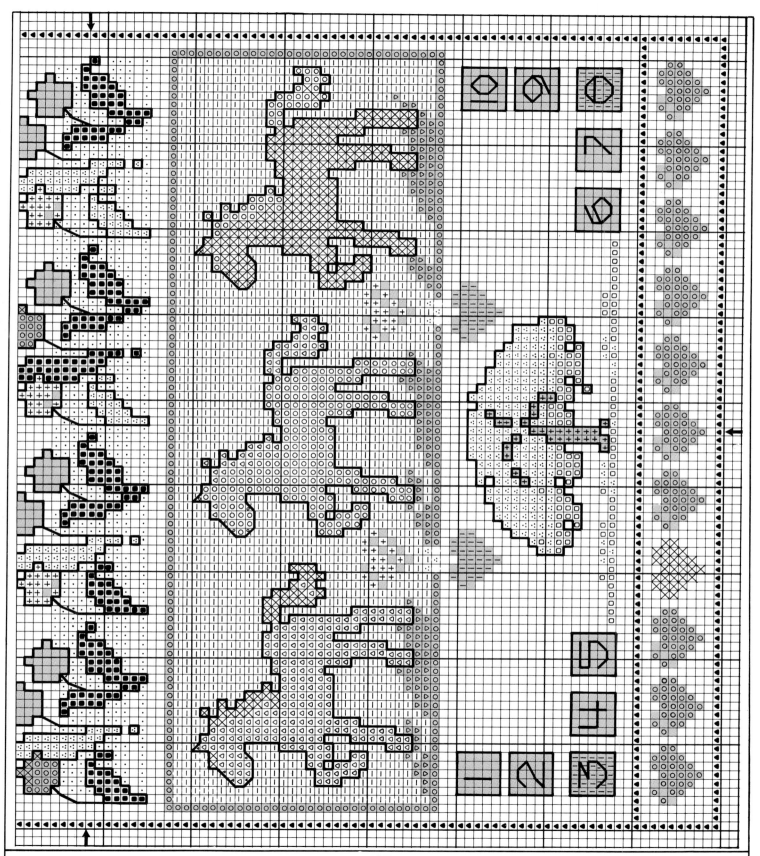

A quilted bunting

Materials needed:

1½ yds. 45" muslin canvas; matching thread
⅞ yd. 45" blue print fabric for lining; matching thread
¼ yd. 45" blue corduroy
¼ yd. 45" tan corduroy
⅛ yd. 45" cranberry corduroy
Batting
Lightweight cardboard for patterns
Dressmaker's pen

A. Prepare fabric:
   1. Preshrink all fabrics.
   2. Make cardboard patterns for large and small triangles, transferring all information.
   3. From canvas, cut one 18½" x 42" piece, one 4" x 42" strip and three 2" x 45" pieces for ties. Also cut 2½" wide bias strips, piecing as needed, to equal 4½ yds. Cut forty-two small triangles, noting grain of fabric.
   4. From blue print fabric, cut one 32" x 42" piece for lining.
   5. From blue corduroy, cut twenty-one large triangles, noting grain of fabric.
   6. From tan corduroy, cut two 2½" x 42" strips.
   7. From cranberry corduroy, cut two 1½" x 42" strips.
   8. From batting, cut one 32" x 42" piece.

Diagram 1

Diagram 2

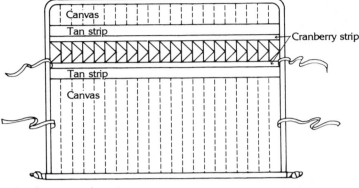

Canvas
Tan strip
Cranberry strip
Tan strip
Canvas

B. Construct bunting:
   1. To finish ties, turn canvas strips inside ½" on each long edge and match folded edges to make strips ½" wide. Top stitch close to both folded edges. Cut two strips in half to make four 22½" ties; do not cut third strip. Set ties aside.
   2. RIGHT sides together, piece triangles with ¼" seams; see Diagram 1. Stitch triangles to make one 4" x 42" strip. Press all seams one direction.
   3. RIGHT sides of triangle strip and one cranberry strip together, stitch with ¼" seam. Repeat with second cranberry strip; see Diagram 2.
   4. RIGHT sides of one tan strip and one cranberry strip together, stitch with ¼" seam. Repeat with second tan strip; see Diagram 2.
   5. RIGHT sides of 18½" x 42" canvas strip and one tan strip together, stitch with ¼" seams. RIGHT sides of 4" x 42" canvas piece and second tan strip together, stitch with ¼" seam. Press all seams one direction.
   6. Place bunting RIGHT side up on flat surface. With dressmaker's pen, mark vertical quilting lines on canvas at 2" intervals and matching seams of triangle strip; see Diagram 2.
   7. Place blue print fabric for lining WRONG side up on flat surface and center batting over it. Center bunting top RIGHT side up over batting and lining. Cut batting and lining to match bunting top. Baste thoroughly.
   8. With matching thread for canvas on spool and matching thread for lining on bobbin, machine quilt on horizontal seams which join corduroy and canvas strips. Machine quilt each vertical pen line.

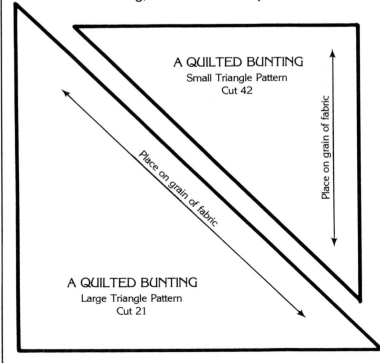

A QUILTED BUNTING
Small Triangle Pattern
Cut 42

Place on grain of fabric

Place on grain of fabric

A QUILTED BUNTING
Large Triangle Pattern
Cut 21

After a long day spent in the country, a child burrows into the warmth of the cozy Quilted Bunting and dreams of the animal pals in the Barnyard Friends Sampler.

9. Place one end of each tie on raw edge of bunting 10" and 20" from top; pin with tie toward center of bunting. Round off corners slightly.

10. RIGHT sides of bias strip and bunting together, stitch through all layers with ½" seam around both sides and top edge, securing ties in seams. Ease additional fullness into bias at corners. Cut bias and set extra aside. Fold bias double to lining, making binding about ⅝" wide; slip stitch.

11. Fold remaining bias strip 2" to WRONG side at each end. RIGHT sides of bias and bottom edge of bunting together, stitch with ½" seam. Fold bias double lining and slip stitch securely, leaving ends open to form casing. Thread remaining strip through casing. To keep tie from pulling out, tack tie through all layers at center back of bunting.

12. Knot ends of all ties. Bunting may be folded and tied or used flat as a quilt.

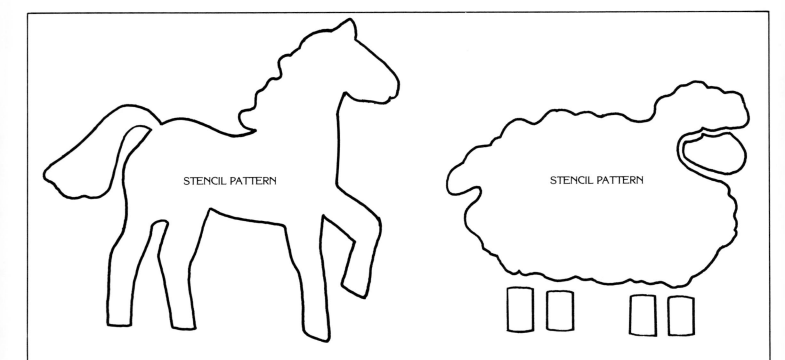

STENCIL PATTERN

STENCIL PATTERN

Shirred sachets

Materials needed:
  ¼ yd. 45" cranberry fabric; matching thread
  Cream wicking cotton or buttonhole twist
  Acrylic paints: green for star, pink for heart
  Stenciling materials; see Stenciling Instructions
  Large-eyed needle
  Stuffing
  Potpourri

1. Make stencil pattern for star or heart; see Stenciling Instructions.
2. From cranberry fabric, cut two 4½" x 4½" pieces for sachet front and back and one 1¾" x 15" piece for backing. Also cut 1¾" wide bias strips, piecing as needed, to equal 1 yd. for shirring.
3. Center and stencil one green star or one pink heart on RIGHT side of one 4½" x 4½" cranberry piece.
4. Sew gathering stitches along both long edges of shirring strip.
5. Gather shirring strip to fit backing piece, distributing fullness evenly. With RIGHT side out, pin shirring strip to backing. Stitch both long edges through all thicknesses with ½" seams.
6. Match short ends with shirring sides together. Stitch ½" seam to make one continuous piece.

7. Divide shirring into quarters and mark. Also mark centers of edges of front and back pieces.
8. RIGHT sides together, match marks on shirring to marks on front piece. Stitch with ½" seam, pivoting at corners. Trim seam allowance to ¼" wide.
9. Repeat Step 8 with second long edge of shirring and back piece, leaving 2" opening in one side.
10. Stuff firmly with stuffing and potpourri. Slip stitch opening closed.
11. Sew Running Stitch on stenciled square ⅜" from seam with single strand of wicking cotton or buttonhole twist, starting at center of one side and leaving 3" tail of cotton; see Diagram 1. Tie 1" wide bow with tails. Knot and trim tails.

Diagram 1

$\mathcal{A}$ pillow pair

Materials needed for one:
- ⅝ yd. 45" print fabric; matching thread
- 12" x 12" piece tan fabric; matching thread
- 1½ yds. medium cording
- Two colors acrylic paints; see photo
- Stenciling materials; see Stenciling Instructions
- 14" x 14" knife edge pillow form

1. From print fabric, cut two 13½" x 13½" pieces for pillow front and back and 1¼" wide bias strips, piecing as needed, to equal 55". Make cording.

2. Center and stencil design diagonally on RIGHT side of 12" x 12" tan piece; see Diagram 1.

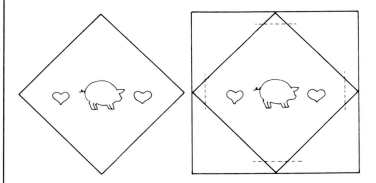

Diagram 1   Diagram 2

3. Turn raw edges of design piece ¼" double to WRONG side and slip stitch.
4. Center design piece diagonally on print piece for pillow front with both RIGHT sides up; see Diagram 2. Baste across points of design piece.
5. Starting in center of bottom edge, pin cording to RIGHT side of pillow front with raw edges matching, rounding corners slightly. Stitch with ¼" seam. Remove basting.
6. RIGHT sides of pillow front and back together, stitch with ¼" seam over stitching line of cording, leaving 8" opening on bottom edge. Turn pillow RIGHT side out.
7. Insert pillow form. Slip stitch opening closed.

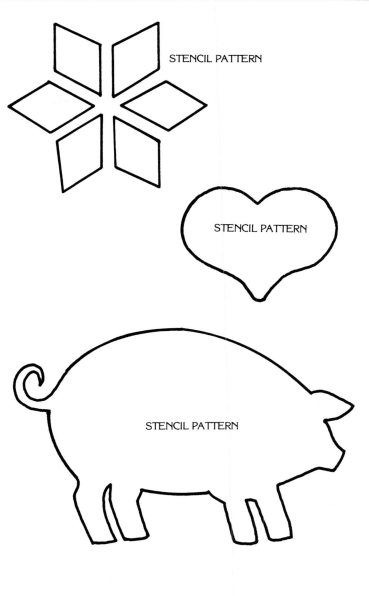

STENCIL PATTERN

STENCIL PATTERN

STENCIL PATTERN

Colorful ribbons and wonderful dolls,
Baskets of hearts and a warm woolen shawl,
Are the magical friends that can always be seen
With November's child and her handful of dreams.

Love is given by The Balloon Woman to her special little friend.

Opposite page: Surrounded by baskets of yarn, a child can nestle in A Shepherd's Afghan and share the afternoon with Andre and Ann Marie, Dolls To Treasure. Childhood secrets are safe with The Balloon Woman. Nearby, Marc and Madeliene from The Friendship Garland wait to join in the play.

Dolls to treasure

ANDRE   LARGE KNIT DOLL

Materials needed:

One 3½ oz. skein each Roly Poly yarn in the following colors: #8001 White, #9512 Gray, #5672 Tan, #6674 Teal Blue, #8107 Pale Teal Blue

Small amounts of #6673 Moss, #9847 Dark Lavender, #74 Light Lavender and #8767 Black yarns

One 50g skein brown mohair yarn for hair

Stuffing

⅝ yd. ⅜" wide dark lavender satin ribbon

Large-eyed needle

One set double-pointed knitting needles, size 3

Gauge: 5 sts = 1"

Knit doll: With gray yarn, cast 80 sts. Divide sts onto 3 needles. Join, being careful not to twist.

Rounds

1- 6:	Purl around
7- 16:	Attach white yarn and work single rib around
17- 18:	Attach teal blue yarn and purl around
19- 36:	Knit
37- 40:	Purl
41- 70:	Attach pale teal blue yarn and knit around
71-100:	Attach tan yarn and knit around

Work decrease rounds in tan yarn as follows:

Round

101:	*K 1, K 2 tog. Repeat from * around end K 2 (54 sts)
102:	Knit around
103:	*K 2 tog, K 1. Repeat from * around (36 sts)
104:	Knit around
105:	*K 1, K 2 tog. Repeat from * around (24 sts)
106:	Knit around
107:	*K 2 tog, K 1. Repeat from * around (16 sts)
108:	Knit around
109:	*K 1, K 2 tog. Repeat from * around end K 1 (11 sts)

Leave 8" of yarn. Thread this yarn onto needle and run through these 11 sts and pull tightly together. Fasten off.

Finishing:

1. Stuff head firmly. Thread one strand of tan yarn through neck stitches. Pull tightly and secure. Stuff body firmly and stitch bottom of feet together with black yarn.

2. With matching yarn, stitch through body with small stitches to form legs.

3. With teal blue yarn, duplicate stitch double rows of stitches for suspenders on front and back, leaving 14 sts between suspenders. With pale teal blue yarn, stitch through body to form arms next to suspenders.

4. With brown mohair yarn, embroider hair with turkey stitch.

5. With black yarn, make double wrap French knots for eyes.

6. With dark lavender yarn, outline stitch parallel lines 1" apart on sleeves. With light lavender and dark lavender yarn, make double wrap French knots for flowers on front of shirt, pants and around sleeves; see photo. With moss yarn, make lazy daisy leaves and outline stitch stems for flowers.

7. With light lavender yarn, duplicate stitch pocket lines on back of pants for hip pockets (8 sts across).

8. Tie dark lavender ribbon in bow around neck.

ANN MARIE   LARGE KNIT DOLL

Materials needed:

One 3½ oz. skein each Roly Poly yarn in the following colors: #8001 White, #9512 Gray, #5672 Tan, #8107 Pale Teal Blue, #9847 Dark Lavender, #74 Light Lavender

Small amounts of #6673 Moss, #6674 Teal Blue and #8767 Black yarns

One 50g skein brown mohair yarn for hair

Stuffing

⅝ yd. ⅜" wide light lavender satin ribbon

1¼ yd. 1/16" wide teal blue satin ribbon

⅜ yd. ½" wide gathered lace

Large-eyed needle

One set double-pointed knitting needles, size 3

Gauge: 5 sts = 1"

Knit doll: With gray yarn, cast 80 sts. Divide onto 3 needles. Join, being careful not to twist.

Rounds

1- 6:	Purl around
7- 12:	Attach white yarn and knit
13- 16:	Attach dark lavender yarn and knit
17- 18:	Attach pale teal blue yarn and knit
19- 28:	Attach dark lavender yarn and knit
29- 30:	Attach pale teal blue yarn and knit
31- 36:	Attach dark lavender yarn and knit
37- 40:	Purl around
41- 70:	Attach light lavender yarn and knit
71-100:	Attach tan yarn and knit around

Work decrease rounds 101-109; see instructions for Andre.

Finishing:
1. Complete Step 1 of Andre.
2. With matching yarn, stitch through shoes and socks to form feet and legs.
3. With dark lavender yarn, duplicate stitch double rows of stitches for suspenders on front and back, leaving 14 sts between suspenders. Duplicate stitch 7 rounds to form bib in front. With light lavender yarn, stitch through body to form arms next to suspenders.
4. With gray yarn, embroider shoe straps with outline stitch; see photo.
5. With pale teal blue yarn, outline stitch parallel lines 1" apart on sleeves. With pale teal blue and teal blue yarns, make double wrap French knots for flowers on bib and sleeves; see photo. With light lavender and teal blue yarns, make double wrap French knots for flowers on skirt; see photo. With moss yarn, make lazy daisy leaves for flowers on bib and sleeves. Make lazy daisy leaves and straight stitch stems for flowers on skirt; see photo.
6. Complete Steps 4 and 5 of instructions for Andre.
7. Slip stitch lace around neck, overlapping ends in back. Cut one 22" length of light lavender ribbon and tie into a bow around neck over lace, tacking as needed to secure.
8. Tie teal blue ribbon in bow around head for headband.

MARC   SMALL KNIT DOLL

Materials needed:
Elsa Williams tapestry wool in the following colors:
    #802 Medium Gray, #900 White, #150 Dark Rose,
    #151 Medium Rose, #713 Tan
Small amounts of #801 Black, #474 Pale Moss, #401 Olive, #153 Light Rose and #822 Medium Blue tapestry wool
Brown mohair yarn for hair
Stuffing
½ yd. ⅛" wide light rose satin ribbon
½ yd. ⅛" wide dark rose satin ribbon
Large-eyed needle
One set double-pointed knitting needles, size 1

Gauge: 7 sts = 1"

Knit body: With medium gray, cast 40 sts on one needle. Divide sts onto 3 needles. Join, being careful not to twist.

Rounds   1- 3: Purl around.
          4- 8: Attach white yarn and work single rib around.
             9: Attach dark rose and purl around
         10-26: Knit
         27-28: Purl

29-30: Attach medium rose and knit around
31-43: Attach dark rose, work 18 sts; add medium rose and knit center 4 sts then with dark rose knit remaining 18 sts. (Keep center 4 sts in medium rose.)
44-58: Attach tan and knit around
   59: K 1, K 2 tog around; end K 1 (27 sts)
   60: K 2 tog, K 1 around (18 sts)
   61: K 1, K 2 tog (12 sts)
   62: K 2 tog, K 1 (8 sts)
   63: K 1, K 2 tog, end K 1 (6 sts) Break yarn 12" and run through all 6 sts

Knit arms: With tan cast 15 sts on one needle. Divide sts onto 3 needles. Join, being careful not to twist.

Rounds   1- 6: Knit around
          7-18: Attach dark rose and knit around
            19: Bind off 4 sts at beginning of row; then knit around (11 sts). Turn.
            20: P 2 tog, P 7 sts, P 2 tog (9 sts)
            21: K 2 tog, K 5, K 2 tog (7 sts)
            22: P 2 tog, P 3, P 2 tog (5 sts)
            23: K 2 tog, K 1, K 2 tog (3 sts)
            24: P, bind off the 3 sts. Leave enough yarn to sew onto body.

Run starting tan yarn tail through cast on sts. Pull tightly and secure. Stuff arms. Sew in place on sides of body. Top of arm should be 1 row down from neck.

Finishing:
1. Stuff head firmly. Thread one strand of tan yarn through neck stitches. Pull tightly and secure. Stuff body firmly and stitch bottom of feet together with gray yarn.
2. With matching yarn, stitch through body with small stitches to form legs.
3. With medium rose yarn, duplicate stitch 3 vertical rows of stitches for band on front of shirt.
4. With brown mohair yarn, embroider hair with turkey stitch.
5. With black yarn, make double wrap French knots for eyes.
6. With pale moss yarn, make lazy daisy stitches for leaves for flowers on front of shirt and around pants; see photo. With light rose yarn, make double wrap French knots for flowers on front of shirt; see photo. With olive and medium blue yarns, make double wrap French knots for flowers around pants; see photo.
7. With olive yarn, make double wrap French knots on top of each sleeve. Also sew straight stitch for pockets on pants.
8. Cut light rose satin ribbon into 2 equal lengths. Tie in bows around wrists.
9. Tie dark rose satin ribbon in bow around neck.

MADELIENE
SMALL KNIT DOLL

Materials needed:

Elsa Williams tapestry wool in the following colors:
#802 Medium Gray, #900 White, #151 Medium Rose, #153 Light Rose, #713 Tan

Small amounts of #801 Black, #150 Dark Rose, #401 Olive, #474 Pale Moss and #601 Dark Lavender tapestry wool

Brown mohair yarn for hair

Stuffing

1 yd. ⅛" wide cranberry satin ribbon

½ yd. ⅛" wide dark rose satin ribbon

Large-eyed needle

One set double-pointed knitting needles, size 1

Gauge: 7 sts = 1"

Knit body: With medium gray, cast 40 sts on one needle. Divide sts onto 3 needles. Join, being careful not to twist.

Rounds	
1-3:	Purl
4-6:	Attach white yarn and knit
7:	Attach medium rose and purl
8-26:	Knit
27-28:	Purl
29-43:	Attach light rose and knit
44-58:	Attach tan and knit
59-63:	Work as for decrease on Marc pattern round 59

Knit arms: Work arms as for Marc pattern using tan for rounds 1-6 and light rose for rows 7 through 24.

Finishing:

1. Complete Step 1 of Marc.
2. With medium rose yarn, duplicate stitch vertical rows of stitches for suspenders on front and back of shirt, leaving 6 sts between suspenders.
3. With dark rose yarn, outline stitch parallel bands on skirt, leaving 7 rows between lines.
4. Complete Steps 4 and 5 of Marc.
5. With pale moss yarn, make lazy daisy stitches for leaves for flowers between bands around skirt; see photo. With light rose and dark lavender yarns, make double wrap French knots for flowers on skirt; see photo.
6. With olive yarn, make lazy daisy stitches for leaves for flowers between suspenders on front of shirt and on top of each sleeve. With pale moss and lavender yarns, make double wrap French knots for flowers on shirt and sleeves.

7. Cut two 9" lengths cranberry ribbon. Tie in bows around wrists. Tie remaining cranberry ribbon in bow around neck.
8. Tie dark rose ribbon in bow around head for headband.

HEART

Materials needed:

Elsa Williams #151 Medium Rose tapestry wool

Stuffing

Large-eyed needle

One set knitting needles, size 1

Gauge: 7 sts = 1"

Knit heart:

With medium rose yarn, cast 3 sts.

Rounds	
1:	P 3
2:	K 1, inc in next 2 sts (5 sts)
3:	P 5
4:	K 1, inc in next st, K 1, inc in next st, K 1 (7 sts)
5:	P 7
6:	K 1, inc 1, K 3, inc 1, K 1 (9 sts)
7-13:	Continue in same manner (inc 2 sts on each side of the K row until 15 sts)
14:	K 7, bind off next st, K 7
15:	Work ½ of the heart, P 7, turn
16:	K 7
17:	P 7
18:	Sl 1, K 1, PSSO, K to last 2 sts then K 2 tog (5 sts)
19:	P
20:	Bind off all 5 sts in K

Break off yarn and attach to center of heart. Work the other half of top of heart by repeating rows 15-20. Leave a 12" yarn tail to whip stitch two heart pieces together. Stuff before closing completely.

Opposite page: Knitting needles and softly colored yarns combine to create The Friendship Garland.

Shepherd's afghan

Materials needed:

11 skeins Scandi Fino Naturwolle (Plymouth)

DMC tapestry wool, art 486, in the following colors and quantities:

#7285 Pale Slate (7 skeins); #7287 Medium Slate (1 skein); #7297 Deep Slate (1 skein); #7221 Pale Mauve (1 skein); #7226 Medium Mauve (2 skeins); #7228 Deep Wine (2 skeins); #7392 Light Moss (3 skeins); #7396 Medium Moss (3 skeins); #7262 Light Wisteria (9 skeins); #7268 Deep Wisteria (3 skeins); #7704 Pale Fern (5 skeins); #7618 Soft Gray (8 skeins).

Size I flexible afghan hook

Size G crochet hook

Gauge: 3 ½ blocks per inch

STEP 1

Center panel: (make 1)

With size I afghan hook, ch 112. Work in afghan st for 117 rows. This will make a total of 112 x 117 blocks. Fasten off.

Corner squares: (make 4)

With size I hook, ch 18. Work in afghan st for 18 rows. Piece will be 18 x 18 blocks. Fasten off.

Panel A: (make 2)

With size I hook, ch 18. Work in afghan st for 117 rows. Piece will be 18 x 117 blocks. Fasten off.

Panel B: (make 2)

With size I hook, ch 112. Work in afghan st for 18 rows. Piece will be 18 x 112 blocks. Fasten off.

STEP 2

Cross-stitch:

Using single strand of DMC tapestry wool, complete cross-stitch on each piece according to graphs.

STEP 3

Single crochet:

Work 1 row sc around each piece, working 1 sc in each block and 3 sc in each corner, ending with slip st in first sc worked.

STEP 4

Shepherd's knot:

ROW 1: With sl st, join yarn to foundation piece at corner. *Draw up loop on hook to ¼", yo and draw through loop on hook. Insert hook between the ¼" loop and the single strand behind it and draw a loop through (2 loops will be on hook). Yo and draw through all loops on hook. (One-half shepherd's knot made.) Repeat from * for other half of knot. Sk 1 sc on foundation row and sc in next sc.

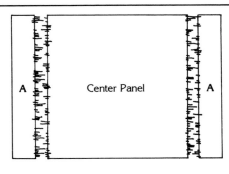

Diagram 1

Center Panel

A   A

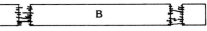

Diagram 2

B

Corner Square

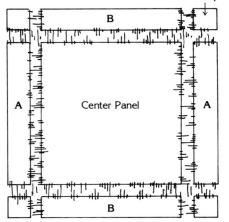

Diagram 3

B

A   Center Panel   A

B

ROW 2: *Work complete knot as in Row 1, anchoring knot as follows: Sc into center sc of last knot worked on previous row. Repeat from * across row. Repeat Row 2 for desired number of rows.

STEP 5

Assembling panels:

ROWS 1-3: Work shepherd's knot along longer side of center panel.

ROW 4: *Work ½ shepherd's knot attaching sc to first sc on longer side of Panel A. Complete shepherd's knot as in previous rows. Repeat from * across, attaching center square to Panel A. Repeat same procedure for opposite side; see Diagram 1.

Attach corner squares to each end of Panel B in like manner, with heart in desired direction. Repeat for second Panel B; see Diagram 2.

Attach Panel B sections to center panel section in like manner; see Diagram 3.

STEP 6

Finishing:

Work 3 rows shepherd's knot around entire afghan to form ruffle.

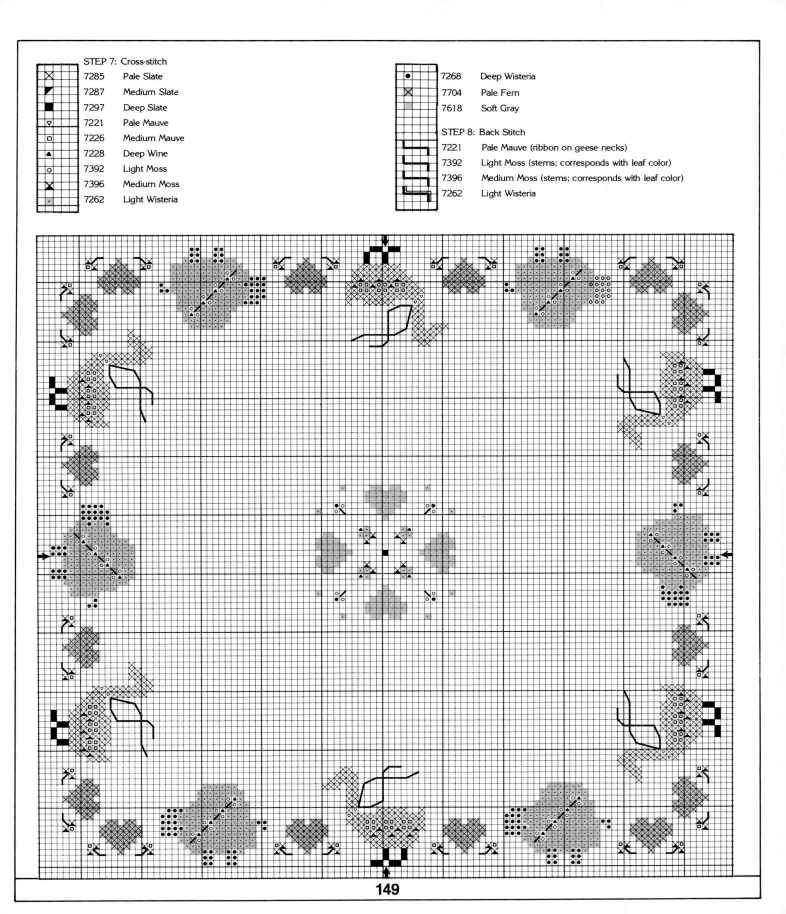

STEP 7: Cross-stitch

☒	7285	Pale Slate
◣	7287	Medium Slate
■	7297	Deep Slate
▽	7221	Pale Mauve
☐	7226	Medium Mauve
▲	7228	Deep Wine
○	7392	Light Moss
☒	7396	Medium Moss
·	7262	Light Wisteria

●	7268	Deep Wisteria
☒	7704	Pale Fern
▨	7618	Soft Gray

STEP 8: Back Stitch

	7221	Pale Mauve (ribbon on geese necks)
	7392	Light Moss (stems; corresponds with leaf color)
	7396	Medium Moss (stems; corresponds with leaf color)
	7262	Light Wisteria

SHEPHERD'S AFGHAN GRAPHS

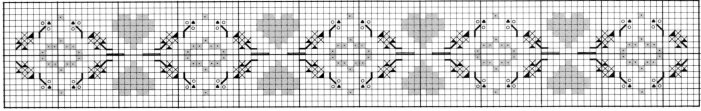

Side Panel

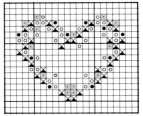

Corner Square

Friendship garland

Materials needed:
   Three completed Madeliene dolls
   Two completed Marc dolls
   Four knitted hearts
   3½ yds. ⅜" wide light rose satin ribbon
   Medium rose yarn to match hearts
   Large-eyed needle

1. Using large-eyed needle threaded with medium rose yarn, stitch together dolls and hearts in order shown in photo.
2. Cut light rose satin ribbon into two equal lengths. Folding one ribbon length in half, knot ribbon at fold. Tack fold to doll's hand at end of garland. Repeat with second ribbon length, tacking at opposite end of garland.

The balloon woman

Cover sample: Stitched on Cream Aida 11. Finished design is 8⅜" x 7⅞". Cut fabric 15" x 14". Finished design sizes using other fabrics are — Aida 14: 6⅝" x 6⅛"; Aida 18: 5⅛" x 4¾"; Hardanger 22: 4⅛" x 3⅞".

BATES		DMC	(used for cover sample)
			Step One: Cross-stitch (three strands)
300	–	745	Yellow · lt. pale
9	□	760	Salmon
44	●	814	Garnet · dk.
105	⊠	209	Lavender · dk.
167	·	519	Sky Blue
921	▨	931	Antique Blue · med.
922	✕	930	Antique Blue · dk.
215	▽	368	Pistachio Green · lt.
216	∴	320	Pistachio Green · med.
246	▲	319	Pistachio Green · vy. dk.
376	○	842	Beige Brown · vy. lt.
403	■	310	Black
			Step Two: Back Stitch (one strand)
246		319	Pistachio Green · vy. dk. (goose's bill)
403		310	Black (all else)
			Step Three: Long Loose Stitch (one strand)
382		3021	Brown Gray · dk. (balloon strings)

The balloon woman

Stitch Count
92
86

December

Angels and gingerbread and wishes of love
Welcome winter's child from a white winged dove.
They are the hope in which we see
Love and peace and blessings for thee.

The stockings, which are indeed Christmas Traditions, are made
with love and filled with tiny gifts, ready for Christmas morning.

Opposite page: Merry, Merry, Merry is the message Santa hummed as he decorated the mantel with the angels and gingerbread men on the
Handmade Ornaments. He has filled Christmas Traditions, in bright green and red, with surprises untold.

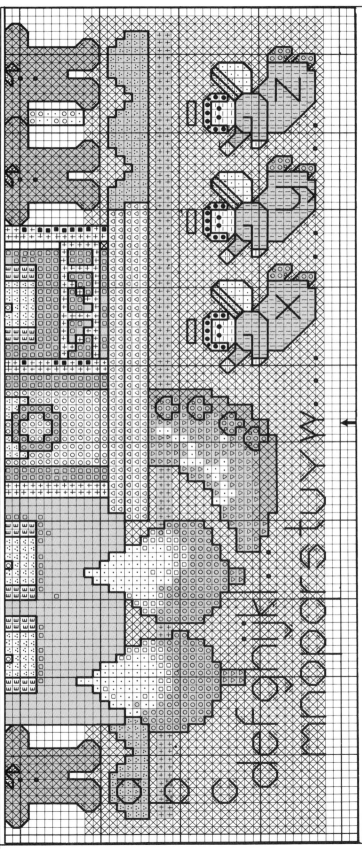

Merry, merry, merry

Cover sample: Stitched on Light Blue Hardanger 22 over two threads. Finished design size is 9½" x 11⅞". Cut fabric 16" x 18". Finished design sizes using other fabrics are — Aida 11: 9½" x 11⅞"; Aida 14: 7½" x 9⅜"; Aida 18: 5⅞" x 7¼"; Hardanger 22: 4¾" x 6".

BATES			DMC	(used for cover sample)
				Step One: Cross-stitch (three strands)
1	·	⁄		White
288	∴	⁄	445	Lemon · lt.
778	–	⁄	948	Peach Flesh · vy. lt.
49	✕	⁄	3689	Mauve · lt.
47	○	⁄	321	Christmas Red
104	I	⁄	210	Lavender · med.
95	+		554	Violet · lt.
99	■		552	Violet · dk.
88	s		718	Plum
158	·		775	Baby Blue · lt.
159	▫		3325	Baby Blue
130			799	Delft · med.
131	▢		798	Delft · dk.
186	+		993	Aquamarine · lt.
187	∵		992	Aquamarine
238	E		703	Chartreuse
229	○	⁄	700	Christmas Green · bright
309	▽	⁄	435	Brown · vy. lt.
371	✕	⁄	433	Brown · med.
382	●	⁄	3371	Black Brown
397	△		453	Shell Gray · lt.
399	▲		452	Shell Gray · med.
				Step Two: Back Stitch (one strand)
88			718	Plum (angel wings)
382			3371	Black Brown (all else)
				Step Three: French Knots (one strand)
382	●		3371	Black Brown

Christmas traditions

Materials needed:

Completed cross-stitch for top band and name band on White Hardanger 22; see cover sample information on page 158

½ yd. 45" print fabric for stocking; matching thread

½ yd. 45" print fabric for lining

Small piece print fabric for binding

½ yd. ⅛" wide dot grosgrain ribbon

⅝ yd. flat white trim

1¾ yds. 1/16" wide satin ribbon to match stocking

1½ yds. 1/16" wide satin ribbon to contrast with stocking

½ yd. polyester fleece

Tracing paper for pattern

A. Prepare fabric:
1. Make pattern for stocking.
2. From fabric for stocking, cut two opposite stockings.
3. From fabric for lining, cut two opposite stockings.
4. From polyester fleece, cut two stockings.
5. From fabric for binding, cut one 2¼" wide bias strips, piecing as needed, to equal 22".

B. Construct stocking front:
1. Trim Hardanger for top border to 3" x 7½" with top of design ½" from top edge of Hardanger. Trim name band to 1¼" with name centered. Zig-zag edges.
2. Place top band 2" from top edge of stocking on RIGHT sides of stocking front piece. Stitch in place.

To make CHRISTMAS TRADITIONS patterns, match dots. (Pattern continued)

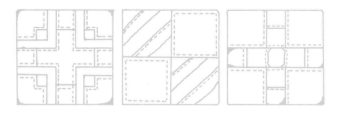
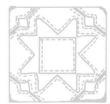

3. Place name band with bottom edge 1¼" from toe on RIGHT side of stocking front piece. Stitch in place.
4. Stitch white trim over edges of Hardanger.
5. From dot grosgrain ribbon, cut two 6½" lengths and one 4½" length. Slip stitch two 6½" lengths ⅛" apart between design and white trim. Slip stitch 4½" length between name and white trim.

C. Construct stocking:
1. Pin fleece pieces to WRONG sides of stocking outside pieces. RIGHT sides of stocking pieces together, stitch with ¼" seam, leaving top edge open. Trim fleece from seam allowance. Turn.
2. With RIGHT sides of lining pieces together, stitch with ¼" seam, leaving top edge open. Turn.
3. Slide lining inside stocking with WRONG side next to fleece and with side seams matching; pin securely.
4. To make loop, cut 4" piece from bias strip. Fold both 4" edges to inside. Fold again and stitch. Pin loop to right seam of lining with raw ends up.
5. RIGHT sides together, place bias next to stocking front around top edge. Stitch with ½" seam. Fold double to lining and slip stitch. Tack loop upright.
6. From satin ribbon which matches stocking, cut one 9" length. Handling remaining matching and contrasting ribbons as one, fold into 3" wide loops. Tie 9" ribbon length around loops to form bow. Tack bow to stocking front between dot grosgrain ribbon lengths; see photo.

Cover sample for "Handmade Ornaments:" Stitched on White Hardanger 22 over two threads. Cut fabric 7" x 7". Center and stitch angel or gingerbread man using colors of floss desired.

Cover sample for "Christmas Traditions" with gingerbread men: Stitched on White Hardanger 22 over two threads. Finished design size is 6⅜" x 1½". Cut fabric 9" x 5". Center and stitch five gingerbread men.

Cover sample for "Christmas Traditions" with angels: Stitched on White Hardanger 22 over two threads. Finished design size is 6⅜" x 1½". Cut fabric 9" x 5". Center and stitch five angels.

Cover sample for "Christmas Traditions" name/monogram bands: Stitched on White Hardanger 22 over two threads with floss to match fabric color. Cut fabric 8" x 4". Compare design size of desired letters with toe section of stocking pattern. Center and stitch letters from "Merry, Merry, Merry" graph, page 154, spacing letters two threads apart.

Handmade ornaments

Materials needed for one:
  Completed cross-stitch on White Hardanger 22; see cover sample information
  One 3" wide styrofoam ball
  Small piece(s) print fabric
  Assorted ribbons
  Pins
  White glue
  Small paring knife

1. Using pencil, draw line around center of ball to divide into two equal halves or draw two parallel lines 1" apart around center of ball.
2. Using paring knife, score lines.
3. To cover back of ball, cut print fabric at least 6½" x 6½". Center and pin fabric.
4. Using paring knife, poke fabric into styrofoam on score line, taking small tucks as needed to mold fabric over round surface. Keep score line as narrow and inconspicuous as possible. Trim excess fabric from edges.
5. On front half, repeat Step 4 with cross-stitch design centered.
6. For ornament with three sections, cut strip 2" x 1". Repeat Step 4.
7. Glue ribbon over score line. Add ribbon bows as desired.

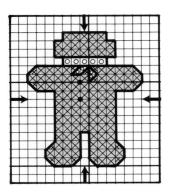
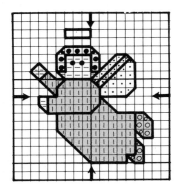

BATES		DMC	(used for cover sample)
		Step One: Cross-stitch (three strands)	
1			White
778		948	Peach Flesh · vy. lt.
47		321	Christmas Red
104		210	Lavender · med.
229		700	Christmas Green · bright
371		433	Brown · med.
382		3371	Black Brown
		Step Two: Back Stitch (one strand)	
88		718	Plum (angel wings)
382		3371	Black Brown (all else)
		Step Three: French Knots (one strand)	
382		3371	Black Brown

Holiday warmers...MITTENS

Materials needed:
  Bucilla Winfant #11 cream
  Small amounts of silver-gray and pink yarn for trim
  ⅝ yd. ⅛" wide lavender satin ribbon
  ¼ yd. 1/16" rose satin ribbon
  Four size 1 double-pointed knitting needles
  One size 18 tapestry needle

  Gauge: 8 sts = 1", 11 rnds = 1"

Thumb: (make 2)
  Cast on 15 sts. Divide onto three needles.
  RNDS 1-14: K. Cut yarn, leaving 12" loose end for sewing. Run a contrasting piece of yarn through sts for yarn holder; set aside.

Mitten:
  Cast on 5 sts. Divide onto three needles.
  RND 1 and all odd rnds: K.
  RND 2: Inc in each st around. (10 sts)
  RND 4: Inc in every other st around. (15 sts)
  RND 6: Inc in every third st around. (20 sts)
  RND 8: Inc in every fourth st around. (25 sts)
  RND 10: Inc in every fifth st around. (30 sts)
  RND 12: Inc in every sixth st around. (35 sts)
  RND 14: Inc in every seventh st around. (40 sts)
  RNDS 15-32: K around. (40 sts)

  With right side facing, sl last 7 sts on thumb to tapestry needle, holding tapestry needle in back of first needle on mitten. Weave first 7 sts of thumb and first 7 sts of next rnd of mitten tog using 12" loose end. Fasten yarn on wrong side. With thumb folded forward, sl rem 8 sts on right end of first needle. K 7, k next 2 sts tog. K around row. (40 sts) K 9 rnds. (40 sts)
  NEXT RND: *K 2 tog. Repeat from * around. (20 sts)
  NEXT 14 RNDS: K loosely. Cut yarn, leaving 18" loose end for sewing.
  Fold 7 rnds to wrong side and sl st each to mitten using 18" loose end.

Finishing:
  Embroider design on back of each mitten; see pattern, page 161.

  Cut two 7" lengths of lavender ribbon. Tie one length into 1½" wide bow. Tack to back of mitten; see photo. Repeat for second mitten.

  Trim rose ribbon to 8½". Handling 8½" length rose ribbon and remaining lavender ribbon as one, tie knot in one end. Tack knot to inside cuff of one mitten. Repeat with second ribbon end and second mitten.

Tiny knitted hats, gloves and mittens, all Holiday Warmers, decorate the tree.

Holiday warmers...GLOVES

Note: Sequence of colors for fingers may be changed as desired.

Materials needed:
   Bucilla Winfant #11 cream
   Phildar Luxe 025 #172 rose
   Phildar Luxe 025 #177 silver-gray
   Phildar Luxe 025 #147 green
   ½ yd. 1/16" or ⅛" wide satin ribbon
   Four size 1 double-pointed knitting needles
   One size 18 tapestry needle

   Gauge: 8 sts = 1", 11 rnds = 1"

LEFT HAND GLOVE:

Index finger:
   Using green yarn, cast on 14 sts. Divide onto three needles.
   RNDS 1-14: K. Run contrasting piece of yarn through sts on last row for yarn holder; set aside.

Middle finger:
   Using cream yarn, cast on 14 sts. Divide onto three needles.
   RNDS 1-18: K. Run contrasting piece of yarn through sts for yarn holder; set aside.

Ring finger:
   Using rose yarn, cast on 14 sts. Divide onto three needles.
   RNDS 1-16: K. Run contrasting piece of yarn through sts for yarn holder; set aside.

Little finger:
   Using silver-gray yarn, cast on 12 sts. Divide onto three needles.
   RNDS 1-12: K. Run contrasting piece of yarn through sts for yarn holder; set aside.

Thumb:
   Using cream yarn, cast on 15 sts. Divide onto three needles.
   RNDS 1-14: K. Run contrasting piece of yarn through sts, leaving 18" loose end for sewing.

Finishing fingers and thumb:
   Run yarn through every other st of cast on edge of fingers and thumb. Pull tightly; fasten.
   Sl 7 green finger sts, 7 cream finger sts, 7 rose finger sts and 6 silver-gray finger sts to one needle.

Glove:
   Using cream yarn, K across 5 sts of green finger. K last 2 green sts and first 2 cream finger sts tog. K 3 more cream sts. K last 2 cream sts and first rose st tog. K 4 more rose sts. K last 2 rose sts and first silver-gray finger st tog. K 5 silver-gray sts. (20 sts) Sl rem silver-gray, rose, cream and green sts to one needle. Divide sts onto three needles.
   Using cream yarn, K 5 silver-gray sts, K last silver-gray st tog with first 2 rose finger sts. K 4 rose sts, K last rose sts and first 2 cream finger sts tog. K 3 cream sts. K last 2 cream sts and first 2 green finger sts tog. K rem green sts. (40 sts) K around for 8 rnds.
   Weave 7 thumb sts to 7 sts on glove, see Diagram 1. With thumb facing, sl rem 8 sts from thumb on right end of left hand needle.
   K 7, K 2 tog, K around on 40 sts for 9 rnds.
   Next Rnd: *K 2 tog. Repeat from * around. (20 sts)
   K 14 rnds loosely.
   Fold 7 rnds to wrong side of glove and sl st each st loosely to glove.
   Using yarn tail of each finger, sew between fingers; fasten off.

RIGHT HAND GLOVE:
   Repeat instructions for left hand glove, reversing thumb and color sequence of fingers.

Finishing:
   Fold ribbon in half. Handling ribbon as one length, tie knot close to fold. Handling both ends as one, tie knot 1" from end. Tack one knot to inside cuff of each glove.

Diagram 1

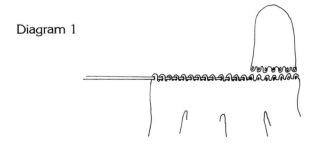

Holiday warmers...HAT

Materials needed for cream hat:
 Bucilla Winfant #11 cream
 Phildar Luxe 025 #147 green for pom-pom
 Small amounts of silver-gray and rose yarn for trim
 ⅜ yd. ⅛" wide lavender satin ribbon
 Four size 1 double-pointed knitting needles
 One size 18 tapestry needle

Materials needed for rose hat:
 Phildar Luxe 025 #172 rose
 Bucilla Winfant #11 cream for pom-pom
 Small amounts of silver-gray and green yarn for trim
 ⅜ yd. 1/16" wide rose satin ribbon
 Four size 1 double-pointed knitting needles
 One size 18 tapestry needle

 Gauge 8 sts = 1", 11 rnds = 1"

Cast on 48 sts. Divide onto three needles. K with fourth needle.
RNDS 1-8: K around.
RND 9: *K 1, sl 1 as to p. Repeat from * around.
RND 10: K around.
RNDS 11-54: Repeat Rnds 9 and 10 (22 times) until 54 rnds from beg have been worked.
RNDS 55-74: K.
RNDS 75-83: Repeat Rnds 9 and 10 (4 times) until 83 rnds from beg have been worked.
RND 84: K 2 tog around (24 sts), leaving 12" loose end for sewing. Thread 12" end onto needle, run through last row of sts and pull to gather top of hat; fasten.

Turn beg cast on sts to inside of hat. Using cream yarn, whip st to last rnd of k 1, sl 1 section.

Finishing:
 Embroider design on front of hat; see pattern. Make 2" pom-pom; see below. Attach pom-pom to top of hat. Tie ⅜ yd. length of ribbon around base of pom-pom for hanging.

EMBROIDERY PATTERN
for hat and mittens

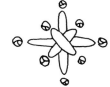

To make pom-pom, cut a strip of cardboard 2" wide. Place one 10" length of yarn along one long edge of cardboard. Wrap remaining yarn loosely around cardboard and 10" length eight times. Slip cardboard out of yarn loops and tie tightly with 10" length of yarn. Clip loops and fluff out; trim ends.

Winter visitors are welcomed by the Braided Wreath in its unique colors and textures.

Braided wreath

Materials needed:
 2 yds. each of three or more heavy fabrics; matching thread
 1½ yds. 45" muslin fabric
 3½ yds. ⅜" wide cream grosgrain ribbon
 10" styrofoam wreath with rounded edges
 Batting
 Dried flowers

1. Cut fabric into 2¾" wide bias strips, piecing as needed, to equal approximately 4 yd. lengths.
2. Fold ⅝" under on both long edges of bias strips. Fold strips in half to measure ⅝" wide. With matching thread, top stitch edges opposite fold.
3. Secure ends of any three strips together and braid so edges with top stitching are hidden as much as possible. Repeat with remaining strips, varying combinations, until braided lengths total at least 34 feet.
4. Wrap layer of batting around wreath and tack; trim excess.
5. From muslin, cut 3" wide bias strips, piecing as needed, to equal 5 feet. Wind bias around wreath; tack.
6. Wrap braid around wreath, placing close together on inside and spreading braid slightly on outside of wreath. Stitch ends together by hand on back of wreath.
7. From ribbon, cut one 30" length; set aside. Cut remaining ribbon into two equal lengths. Wrap one length around bottom of wreath twice and tie bow; see photo. Repeat with second length ribbon. With 30" length, tie bow and tack with first two bows. Add dried flowers.

General instructions

CROSS-STITCH

FABRICS: Most fabrics used in this book are evenweave fabrics made especially for cross-stitch and are available in needlework departments or shops. Fabrics used in the models in the photographs are identified in the cover sample information by color, name and thread count per inch.

NEEDLES: Use a blunt tapestry needle which slips easily through holes in fabric and does not pierce fabric. With fabric having eleven or fewer threads per inch, use needle size 24; with fourteen threads per inch, use needle size 24 or 26; with eighteen threads or more per inch, use needle size 26.

PREPARING FABRIC: Cut fabric 3" larger on all sides than design size or cut as indicated in cover sample information. To keep fabric from fraying, whip stitch or machine zigzag raw edges.

HOOP OR FRAME: Select frame or stretcher bars large enough to hold entire design. Place screw or clamp of hoop in 10 o'clock position (or 2 o'clock, if left handed) to keep from catching.

FLOSS: Cut floss into 18" lengths. For best coverage, run floss over damp sponge and separate all six strands of floss. Put back together number of strands recommended for use in cover sample information. Floss will cover best when lying flat. If twisted, drop needle and allow floss to unwind.

CENTERING DESIGN: Find center of fabric by folding from top to bottom and again from left to right. Place pin in point of fold to mark center. Locate center of graph by following vertical and horizontal arrows. Begin stitching at center point of graph and fabric. Each square on graph represents one complete cross-stitch. Unless indicated otherwise in cover sample information, each stitch is over one unit of thread.

SECURING FLOSS: Never knot floss unless working on clothing. Hold 1" of thread behind fabric and secure with first few stitches. To secure end of thread, run under four or more stitches on back of design.

READING GRAPHS: To help distinguish colors in designs, shade graphs with colored pencils.

BACK STITCHING: Complete all cross-stitches before working back stitches or accent stitches. When back stitching, use number of strands indicated in code or one strand fewer than used for cross-stitch.

STITCHING METHOD: Use "push and pull" method for smoothest stitch. Push needle straight down and completely through fabric before pulling up.

CARRYING FLOSS: Do not carry floss more than ½" between stitched areas. Loose threads, especially dark ones, will show through fabric. When carrying floss, run under worked stitches on back side when possible.

CLEANING COMPLETED WORK: After making sure fabric and floss are colorfast, briefly soak completed work in cold water. If soiled, wash gently in mild soap. Roll work in towel to remove excess water; do not wring. Place work face down on dry, lightweight towel and, with iron on warm setting, press until work is dry.

STEP 1: Cross-Stitch — Bring needle and thread up at A, down at B, up at C, and down again at D; see Diagram 1. For rows of cross-stitch, stitch across entire row so floss is angled from lower left to upper right, then return; see Diagram 2. ALL STITCHES MUST LIE IN THE SAME DIRECTION.

Diagram 1   Diagram 2

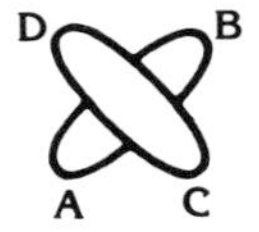

Half-Cross — Indicated on graph by slanted line with color symbol beside it (see Diagram 1), make longer stitch in direction of slanted line.

Diagram 1

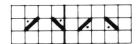

The stitch actually fits three-fourths of the area; see Diagram 2. Bring needle and thread up at A, down at B, up at C, and down at D.

Diagram 2

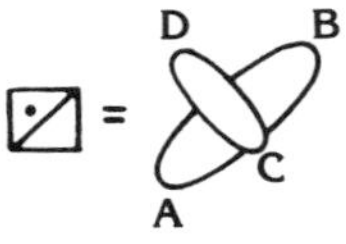

In cases where two colors meet, the graph will be similar to Diagram 3. The stitched area will look like Diagram 4.

Diagram 3   Diagram 4

STEP 2: Back Stitch — Working from left to right with one strand of floss (unless designated otherwise in code), bring needle and thread up at A, down at B, and up again at C. Going back down at A, continue in this manner; see Diagram 1.

Diagram 1

STEP 3: French Knot

STEP 4: Bead Work — Attach beads to fabric with a half-cross, lower left to upper right. Secure beads by returning thread through beads, lower right to upper left. Complete row of half-crosses before returning to secure all beads.

Perforated paper available from
  Astor Place
  239 Main Avenue
  Stirling, NJ 07980

Ribbon available from
  C.M. Offray and Son, Inc.
  261 Madison Avenue
  New York, NY 10016

Fabrics available from
  Joan Toggitt
  35 Fairfield Place
  West Caldwell, NJ 07006

KNITTING AND CROCHETING STITCHES

Afghan stitch

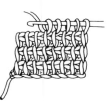

Cross-stitch on afghan stitch

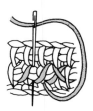

Duplicate stitch

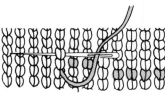

Turkey stitch

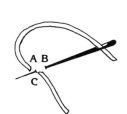

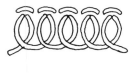

EMBROIDERY STITCHES

Blanket or buttonhole stitch

Couching stitch

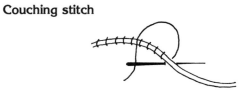

Lazy daisy stitch

Outline stitch

Running and quilting stitch

Satin stitch

Straight stitch

Chevron stitch

Chained feather stitch

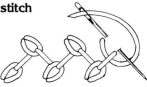

Herringbone stitch

STENCILING INSTRUCTIONS

PREPARATION: Select moderate or tight weave natural fabric without nap. Preshrink all fabrics; press.

SUPPLIES: Acrylic paint; stiff brush with ½" bristles; stencil board (available at art supply store); X-Acto knives or single edged razor; small containers for mixing paints; water for cleaning brushes; tracing paper; carbon paper; pencil; dressmaker's pen.

MAKING PATTERNS: Cut pieces of stencil board at least 1" larger on all sides than design. Copy entire pattern onto stencil board once for each color being used. With X-Acto knife, cut one template for each color. Cut smaller areas first. Once started cutting, rotate stencil board and follow the design clockwise (if righthanded). Do not lift the knife or razor blade until that line of the design is completed.

COLORS: Acrylic paints come in a variety of colors but may need to be mixed to achieve desired shade to match fabrics being used. Mix enough of a color to complete the project; it is very difficult to match a color later. Use small containers for mixing colors. Acrylic paint as it comes from the tube is a good consistency for fabric stenciling. Add only a few drops of water if needed.

APPLYING PAINT: Pin, tape or staple fabric to flat surface to keep it taut. Position stencil. Begin working at top of design and work down. Use small amounts of paint and a nearly dry brush. Dab the paint, applying it first to the edges of the design, then the center, covering the entire area evenly. Allow to dry, then using next template, apply second color.

CLEANING: Iron the stenciled work from the WRONG side. Hand wash in cold water and do not wring. Dry flat.

SEWING HELPS

CIRCLE PATTERN INSTRUCTIONS: To make circle pattern, tie string around pencil. Measure half the width of circle from pencil. Tie knot in string at that point. Place knot in center of paper and hold with thumb. Move pencil in circle. Check measurements and correct irregularities.

TOPSTITCHING: Topstitching is used as an accent on top of fabric where it shows. The stitching should be uniform and is usually parallel to a seam or part of design.

BASTING: Basting stitches are done by hand to temporarily hold layers of fabric and fleece or batting in a particular position. Remove stitches once project is complete. Basting stitches are usually sewn with a contrasting color of thread which is easy to see, but which will not leave marks. Some dark colors leave a trail.

BIAS STRIPS: Bias strips are used for ruffles, binding or cording. They are always cut diagonally at a 45-degree angle to the grain of the fabric. To cut bias, fold fabric diagonally and crease. Pin and cut at fold. Cut additional strips the width indicated in instructions and parallel to first cutting line. Cut ends of bias on grain of fabric. Place RIGHT sides together and stitch ends with ¼" seam. Continue to piece strips until length indicated in instructions.

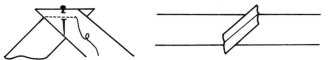

CLIPPING SEAMS: Clipping seam allowances is necessary on all curves, points and most corners so finished seam will lie flat. Clip into seam allowance at even intervals ¼" to ½" apart, being careful not to cut through stitching.

CORDING (also called welting or piping): Piece bias strips together (see Bias Strips) to equal length needed for cording. Place cord in center of WRONG side of strip and fold fabric over it. Using zipper foot, stitch close to cord through both layers of fabric. Trim seam allowance to ¼" from stitching line.

GATHERS: Machine stitch two parallel rows of long stitches ¼" and ½" from edge of fabric (unless instructions indicate differently). Leave ends of thread 2" or 3" long. Pull two bobbin threads and gather to fit length indicated. Long edges may need to be gathered from both ends. Disperse fullness evenly and secure threads in seam by wrapping around pin in figure-eight.

SLIP STITCHING: Slip stitching (or blind stitching) is used to join two pieces of fabric by hand and provides an almost invisible finish. Insert needle at A, slide ⅛" to ¼" through folded edge of fabric and bring out at B. Directly below B, take small stitch through second piece of fabric.

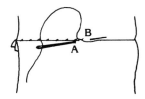

Index

For information on how you can have *Better Homes and Gardens* delivered to your door, write to: Mr. Robert Austin, P.O. Box 4536, Des Moines, IA 50336.